DESERT SURVIVAL
HANDBOOK

How to Prevent and Handle Emergency Situations

by Charles A. Lehman

D0950573

Desert Survival Handbook
How to Prevent and Handle Emergency Situations
by Charles A. Lehman

Published by American Traveler Press
5738 North Central Avenue
Phoenix, Arizona 85012
(602) 234-1574
info@AmericanTravelerPress.com

©1993, 1998 by Primer Publishers

Sixth Printing 2003, Revised

All rights reserved. No part of this book may be reproduced in any form or by any means, except for review purposes, without written permission of the publisher.

Printed in the United States of America.

ISBN 0-935810-65-X

Cover and interior design: The Printed Page

Publisher's Cataloging-in-Publication
(Provided by Quality Books, Inc.)

Lehman, Charles A.
     Desert survival handbook : how to prevent and handle
emergency situations / by Charles A. Lehman. — 2nd ed.,
rev.
     p. cm.
     Includes index.
     ISBN: 0-935810-65-X

     1. Desert survival—Handbooks, manuals, etc. 2. Survival
skills—Handbooks, manuals, etc.   I. Title.

GV200.5.L44 1998   613.6′9
                                    QBI98-661

Contents

Survival? Who Needs It?

It won't happen to me

"Desert survival? Who needs it? Nothing's ever happened to me."
"I never get more than a few miles from a main highway. What do I care about survival?" These are some typical responses heard on the subject of this book.

Okay, you need the skills outlined here *only* if you:

- ▲ Drive through deserts
- ▲ Backpack in the desert
- ▲ Fish desert reservoirs
- ▲ Fly a light plane
- ▲ Hang glide
- ▲ Live near a desert
- ▲ Hike in the desert
- ▲ Watch desert birds
- ▲ Hunt in the desert
- ▲ Ride horseback

People tend to think survival is a primitive "live-off-the-land" skill needed by explorers. Most assume that since they don't fit into that category they don't need the skill.

Survival is really nothing more than managing your own mind and body in an unusual or hostile environment—and you can find yourself in that position, no matter who you are or what you do.

Suppose you are driving from El Paso to Phoenix along Interstate 10. About noon the utter boredom of freeway driving and the haunting beauty of the desert tempt you to take a "short-cut." You take the first exit, drive south about five miles, then turn west on a well-maintained road. Paralleling the freeway is much more pleasant, and your air conditioner keeps you in perfect comfort as mile after mile of colorful desert rolls by.

You check the rearview mirror to insure that this magnificent scenery is yours alone. No cars behind—but there is a white cloud billowing out behind your car. The bright red "HOT" light flashes on the instrument panel. Blown radiator hoses are common in the best of cars.

A blast of oppressive heat almost takes your breath away as you step from the driver's seat. One of the local radio stations mentioned a temperature of 115° just before you shut off the overheated engine.

But it feels much hotter. In the last hour you passed one ranch—about twenty-five minutes back—and met two cars just after you left the freeway.

You are only about five miles from the freeway, but you're quite isolated. This is a bona fide survival situation growing out of everyday life. How would you insure your survival in the searing desert heat? Select the one best answer.

- ❑ a. Begin walking toward the freeway and hail a passing car.
- ❑ b. Strip off as many clothes as possible to help beat the heat, then walk slowly back down the road looking for help.
- ❑ c. Stay in your car.
- ❑ d. Get in the shade, wait until dark, then walk out.

The answer is d. You'll find the reasons in Chapters 2 and 3. Survival situations can and do happen to average folks, as well as to adventurous explorers. You have the capacity to handle these situations if you know and follow the basic principles of survival.

This book will get you started. The basics are here. As you project yourself into the scenarios, play the role, and you will find it's fun to learn about desert survival.

Finally, carry this book in your backpack, car, boat, airplane, or saddlebag as an extra confidence factor—a security blanket. If you should have a problem, it will be a handy reference as you wait for rescue, the weather to clear, or the cool of the desert evening.

Your Body Is Where You Live

Desert survivors face many hazards, but only four present any immediate danger—heat, cold, dryness and injuries. If you enter your personal survival situation without getting hurt or asphyxiated, there are only three conditions which can pose immediate threats to your life (managing injuries is a separate subject and is covered in Chapter 12).

Hyperthermia, dehydration, and hypothermia are the three dangers. Prevent them and you are going to come home little the worse for wear. All three boil down to taking care of your body—that is where you live.

Your body is something like the engine in your car. Supply it with the proper fuel, adequate cooling and efficient lubricants and it will run for years. Neglect any one of these and you are headed for trouble.

Hyperthermia, or overheating your body can be as disastrous as "over-temping" your car's engine—both can cause seizure of the machine. Fortunately, your body has a marvelous cooling system, capable of keeping your temperature stabilized around 99 degrees, even in the hottest desert. It can be overtaxed, though, unless you are careful.

Food heats your body; perspiration, breathing, and radiation cool it.

Let's say you were on an early morning hike in the desert west of Las Vegas, about ten miles off Interstate 15. You get disoriented. It is now noon and the temperature is 120°. You are in no immediate danger—but wrong moves can do you in.

Naturally, you are eager to get back to civilization and the excitement and tables of Las Vegas. However, if you rush around trying to find your way or set out for the highway, you can easily overtax your cooling system. If you work so hard that most of your sweat is running off rather than evaporating, your temperature will begin to rise. As it

HYPERTHERMIA

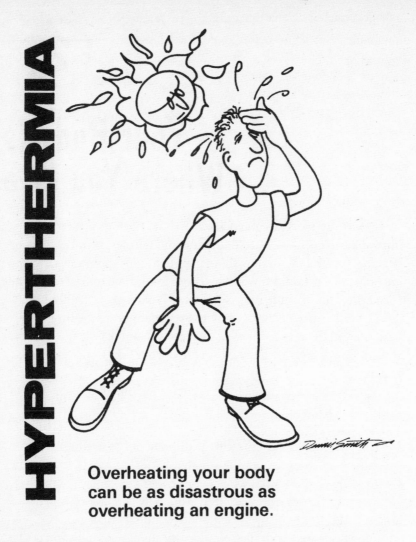

Overheating your body can be as disastrous as overheating an engine.

does, your body's heat-regulating mechanism in the brain ceases to function and you stop sweating. Your skin flushes and becomes dry. Suddenly, you collapse—the classic "heat stroke." Without treatment, death may follow.

It's quite obvious that you cannot treat your own heat stroke. You have to *prevent* your temperature from getting too high. In hot weather that means severely limiting your physical activity, wearing your clothing loosely (but wearing it), staying in the shade, and drinking plenty of water.

The trouble is, survival conditions can impose serious limitations on your ability to do these things. You may have to build your own shade and you may not have "plenty of water." Still, you should be aware of the danger of heat and keep heat management high on your list of priorities.

Although heat stroke is the most dangerous form of hyperthermia, heat can also cause other problems unless you act to *prevent* them.

Heat cramps can be painful and disabling. They are not true hyperthermia, because your body temperature may still be normal when they occur. If you have been working hard and sweating a lot, you are losing more than water. Even if your body can maintain its temperature, it will deplete its supply of water and salts (also called electrolytes, because when dissolved in water they form the conductive medium for electrical nerve impulses). You may drink plenty of water, but unless you also take in food or salt, the change in electrolyte balance may cause your muscles to cramp.

In a survival situation, you avoid cramps the same way you prevent true hyperthermia—by staying out of the sun and resting as much as possible. Sweat and salts are difficult to replace under survival conditions, so consider each a precious resource—too valuable to waste.

Perspiration is the common thread that ties together two of your immediate survival hazards: overheating and **dehydration**. Your body sweats to prevent hyperthermia, but even when it is successful, it dehydrates itself in the process. Unless you control this dehydrating effect, you can cause yourself an awful lot of grief.

Picture yourself stranded in a desert area during winter. You scurry around all day building a snug shelter for yourself and your companion. Both of you have worked hard on the lean-to and gathered firewood for the night; you were smart enough to avoid getting your clothes wet with sweat by stripping off a layer or two as you worked. Around noon you each ate one of the sandwiches you had packed for the trip.

In the evening your cheerful fire and cozy shelter have you feeling pretty good. "This survival business isn't bad at all. We're comfortable for tonight, and tomorrow there's sure to be someone out looking for us." Your partner does not answer and seems unusually quiet. "Bill, what's the matter—you look sick." Bill doesn't look up, but mutters, "Yeah, it's my stomach. I feel like I'm going to lose that sandwich—and that's all the food we've got."

If you were stranded during the summer, you might suspect Bill's problem—and yours. It is water, or rather the lack of it.

Dehydration is the culprit. Working vigorously in the dry air, you and Bill were perspiring, but you did not notice because your sweat evaporated quickly. Every breath you exhaled took some water vapor with it. Those beef sandwiches were delicious and good for you, but the few sips of thermos coffee you washed them down with did nothing to help. Digesting the protein in the beef took far more fluid from your body than the coffee added.

You need a minimum of 3 quarts of water daily

DEHYDRATION

A LOSS OF 5% OR MORE OF YOUR BODY WATER IS DANGEROUS.

Dehydration is sneaky. There are early symptoms of the problem, but you are not apt to notice them if you are busy. A feeling of thirst is a very unreliable indicator. Oh, you'll get thirsty all right as you start to dehydrate. The problem is that just a few sips will often quench the thirst without improving your internal water deficit. Or you may not notice the thirst in the first place because you are distracted. Being marooned in strange surroundings can be quite distracting.

If your natural thirst fails to spur you to drink enough water to rebalance your electrolytes, you will probably begin to notice a rather vague discomfort—again, not unusual for a survivor. As you use up more of your body's water, you will find it is more comfortable to move slowly or not at all than to hustle about your chores. If you glanced in a mirror, you'd notice your skin was a bit red, but you probably would pass that symptom off as sunburn or windburn. You will become impatient, too; but who wouldn't with no rescue in sight. So you still have no reliable indicator that all is not well.

Loss of appetite along with increased pulse and respiration will also occur, but you're not likely to notice because your isolated situation may trigger the same responses.

At a water loss of about five percent of your body weight, you will get sick—just plain miserable. Waves of nausea will destroy all desire to drink. If you vomit, you will lose additional quantities of water. Then things start downhill in a hurry. You are losing fluid, you can't or won't drink, and the symptoms get worse.

As water loss continues, more noticeable symptoms will begin to appear. You may get dizzy, develop a severe headache, become short of breath, experience tingling extremities, a dry mouth, "thick" speech and become unable to walk. Dehydration at this level is extremely dangerous. You have to *prevent* it.

In a desert survival episode, water may be scarce or nonexistent. If so, your safest bet is to be extremely stingy with the supply stored inside you. There is little you can do to reduce some water losses. You will lose almost two quarts of water each day through urination, breathing, and bowel movements. If you eat, more water will be used to digest the food. Eating is controllable. So is the other big water thief—sweating. When you're a survivor, perspiration is your enemy. It robs you of the water supply stored in your body and fouls up your electrolytic balance.

If you have water—drink it, don't ration or save it. People have died in the desert with water in their canteens. They rationed that water while their bodies dehydrated and quit working for them.

Unless you have lots of water available, eat sparingly and don't work up a sweat. Read more about water in Chapters 6 and 8.

The third hazard, **hypothermia**, is a lowering of the body's core temperature. You are designed to operate at about 99 degrees Fahrenheit. Drop that temperature even a few degrees and the machine starts to break down.

The desert cools off rapidly as soon as the sun sets. Suppose you have a flat tire at night on a lonely road. While you are struggling with the spare, a soft rain starts. There is a wind coming up, too. By the time you discover the spare is flat, you're soaked.

Eventually, another car stops to pick you up; by then, you are shaking like a leaf. You have never felt so cold. That's hypothermia—the newspapers call it "exposure."

You have probably experienced hypothermia at this level many times, so what's the big deal? Well, in a survival situation hypothermia can be a killer—and a sneaky one at that.

Let's suppose no one comes by to pick you up. When you start to shiver, your body is sending a desperate signal. "Cover me up and feed me, I'm getting cold!"

Your body, like an engine, generates both energy and heat as it burns fuel. When you start to shiver, the body is telling you it is losing calories (heat) faster than they are being replaced. The shivering reflex exercises a whole bunch of muscles, and increases heat production by burning more fuel. The fuel in this case is food.

Shivering alone is not likely to rewarm you. Active *prevention* is the key. If you have dry clothes, put them on. To produce heat you can run in place or do calisthenics or isometrics. This forces your muscles to burn more fuel and that generates heat.

But in some survival situations, if you opt to exercise, you are burning fuel you can't easily replace or you may not have dry clothes to put on. Under survival conditions you have to *prevent* hypothermia. Failing that, you must act fast. That means reducing heat loss as much as possible with a shelter, fire, and more clothing.

This seems fairly straightforward. But see what happens if you are slow to react or don't know what to do.

HYPOTHERMIA

THE LOWERING OF THE BODY'S CORE TEMPERATURE

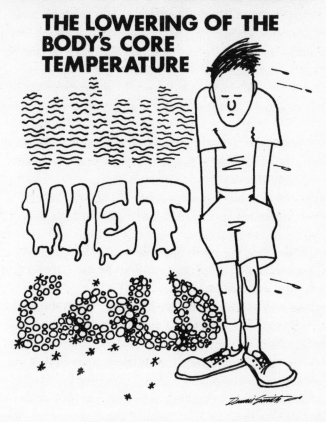

While you are shivering, the circulation to your hands and feet is being choked off. That is another automatic reflex to keep your vital organs warm. By reducing the flow of blood to your extremities, your body is reducing its loss of heat. But your hands and feet will get cold and stiff.

The last thing you need in a tight situation is clumsy hands. Those hands are going to have to build a fire, put up shelter, or button a coat. Ever try to strike a match with fingers stiff from cold?

As your core temperature continues to drop, you'll stop shivering. That is a sure danger sign—and one you are not likely to recognize, because the biggest danger of hypothermia is that it takes away your will to help yourself. Amazing as it may seem, about the time you quit shivering you also quit worrying. You are dying and you couldn't care less.

At this point, your body has lost the ability to rewarm itself. So, even if you have unlimited clothing or a thick sleeping bag to crawl into, you will continue to cool off. That means your only hope is adding heat. It could come from a warming fire, hot drinks—or another human body.

It is vital in a survival situation to *prevent* hypothermia, or at least to recognize it very early. You may not have a sleeping bag or a warm partner.

Prevent hypothermia by constantly thinking of your body as a heat producer with a limited supply of fuel. Use every means available to insulate yourself and stay dry!

If you have extra clothing with you, put it on before you start to shiver. Don't sit on or lean against rocks or metal vehicle parts. You'll lose heat very rapidly through conduction. Get a fire going at the first hint of a chill. If possible, use more than one fire, so you can add heat from both sides. Drink all the hot fluids you can swallow. If you have extra food, use it to refuel and keep your body furnace going.

One final note on hypothermia—alcohol is not a useful fuel. Your body will burn alcohol, but at the same time it will short circuit that automatic reflex which reduces blood flow to your extremities. As a result, just when your body is trying desperately to keep all that warm blood in close, near your vital organs, alcohol is opening the flood gates to your face, hands and feet. To make matters worse, alcohol slows your body processes—like generating heat. You will feel warm, but you'll lose heat very fast, and your heart, lungs, and other internal organs will chill and quit. You may feel warm while you are dying. No alcohol!

Protecting your body from hyperthermia, dehydration and hypothermia is your most critical challenge. You do it by managing your body as though it were a precious spacecraft engine with very limited fuel, coolant and lubricant—the only engine that can get you home.

Take Cover

Learning the skills of finding or building a shelter is easy. Let's go back to the desert drive described in Chapter 1. You've got to get out of that blazing sun, or you're a prime candidate for hyperthermia or dehydration. Walking five miles to the Interstate would be an endurance contest you'd likely lose. Stripping off your clothes will only make matters worse. They're part of your shelter. Stay close to the car and get into the shade. You can walk out in the cool of the night.

It's just after noon, so the car casts a narrow shadow that's not really big enough to shade you. However, you note a scraggly tree and a rock ledge nearby that offer larger patches of shade. Checking under the tree, you discover the ground is very hot, even in the shade. The moving shade allows the sun to bake the ground. Sitting there would be uncomfortable. You could use the tree shade if you could remove the back seat or spare tire of your car to sit on. Or you might dig down a few inches to cooler soil. Your tire jack and hub caps are good digging tools. Be lucky and find a north-facing rock ledge that casts an all-day shadow. You wisely decide to rest in the best available shade until after sunset.

Okay, that was an easy one—but it illustrates some basic principles of shelters. Learn them, and all the rest will fall in line:

1. Recognize the need for shelter.
2. Take advantage of natural protection.
3. Make provisions for heating or cooling.
4. Conserve your energy. (Don't build a log cabin when a lean-to will do.)

All shelters have one basic purpose—to protect your body from overheating, overcooling or drying out. In other words, they prevent hyperthermia, hypothermia and dehydration.

We'll look at two types of shelters: natural shelters of opportunity and improvised shelters you build.

Most obvious in the natural class are vehicles. Probably more people get into "survival" situations while using vehicles than by all other means combined. Cars, boats, and airplanes all make very good shelters—under certain, limited circumstances. If they have fuel, are in running order, and have unobstructed exhaust systems, they can be excellent for general use. However, once the engine is dead they all have serious drawbacks. They are hard to heat and impossible to cool because they offer little insulation. On the other hand, they are relatively rainproof and windproof.

If wind or rain is your primary environmental threat, by all means use your car, boat, or plane. Unfortunately, the shade you get inside your car is of little help; it's like a shady oven. Use the shade outside your car. Depending on the sun's angle, that may mean crawling under the vehicle—no easy task on some low-slung models. There is usually some place to squeeze underneath. Use a hub cap to dig away a few inches of dirt. Watch out for hot exhaust pipes. Airplanes, too, are better ovens than shade trees, but it is usually easy to use wings or tail surfaces for protection from the sun.

On the shores of our Southwestern desert lakes the combination of shade from a disabled boat and cooling from the lake water (splashed onto your clothes) almost eliminates the hazard of desert heat. Again, the only safe survival decision is to stay with the boat and use its shelter and equipment.

Man-made "shelters" dot the sides of nearly every road. Barns, cattle shelters, abandoned houses, or even houses whose owners are away have all saved overheated, tired, wet or cold travelers.

In 1976 I took part in the search for a mentally retarded, fifteen year old boy who had wandered away from an outing. The weather was terrible—cold rain and wind. Conditions were perfect for hypothermia, and this lad had the mental age of a two year old, so we expected the worst. All night about one hundred searchers combed half a dozen square miles of Southwestern rangeland without success. By dawn, hope was fading for the lightly clad boy. Then he was found, asleep, dry and warm. When the rain started, he'd crawled into the hay inside an old barn. His natural inclination to curl up and go to sleep when he got cold had saved him.

Most people would have been embarrassed at being lost so close to home and probably would have tried to walk out, getting soaked and hypothermic in the process. Sometimes, man-made structures can provide all the protection you need in any weather if you will just admit you need shelter, and exercise your ingenuity to find and use it.

Culverts and bridges can provide shelter along roads or railroads. Naturally, some of them are so located as to be subject to flash flooding. If you must seek shelter under a bridge or in a culvert, stay alert and have an escape route planned if water should begin rising dangerously.

Caves and rock overhangs make excellent shelters from heat, cold, wind, or water. They provide cool shade in the desert, and when equipped with a proper fire, they can be almost permanent shelters—which apparently they were for a considerable part of man's history. One of the best night's rest I ever had was on the sandy floor of a 10-by-40-foot rock cave. It faced west, and the afternoon sun had warmed the sand and rock, which stayed warm all night and kept me comfortable.

In spite of their comfort and natural attraction, caves demand a bit of caution. Watch out for caves or holes in sandy or gravel banks. They have a habit of collapsing during wet weather. The same goes for caves or overhangs with loose rocks overhead. If you are in a predicament that calls for using a cave as shelter, you are not on a cave exploration jaunt. Don't go beyond sight of the entrance!

Again, a word of caution. It's nice to have company in a survival situation—but before you plunge into some cozy cavity, check it out. Sometimes the "critters" that live there would not make good roommates. You may be able to evict them, but be careful what you try to displace and how you go about it.

An entire book this size could be devoted to improvised shelters, because there are an almost unlimited number of styles and modifications. So we'll limit this discussion to a few easy-to-build styles which can be modified to suit the weather, terrain or personal whims.

One of the easiest and most versatile of all shelters is the simple lean-to. It can be built of almost any material, in a variety of situations. A well-built lean-to will provide a dry, roomy shelter that can be heated with a fire. You can build a lean-to with no tools or man-made materials, but it is easier if you always carry a few yards of cord, a knife and a sheet of plastic.

A lean-to is nothing more than a steeply-sloping roof (about 60°) that extends all the way to the ground. It may have sides if you wish. You can build one from poles, cover it with sage brush, blankets, floor mats, the hood from your car, poncho, or raincoat. Lacking poles, you can support your lean-to from the side of your car, a cactus, rocks, etc.

Lean-tos are fast, easy and adaptable. The roof should be steep enough to shed rain, high enough to let you sit comfortably, and wide enough so you can stretch out parallel to the entrance if you are alone or from front to back if you have company. Place the rear of the lean-to against the wind, so you can put a fire in front without worrying about smoke. If there is a significant wind, close in the rear.

You can get as fancy as you like with a lean-to, but remember, the reason you are building the shelter is to conserve and preserve the energy you are carrying within you—so don't waste energy building a fancy shelter. However, try to avoid sitting or lying on the sun-baked ground. A crude but protective shelter covering a rested and healthy body is far better than a textbook-perfect shelter containing an exhausted survivor.

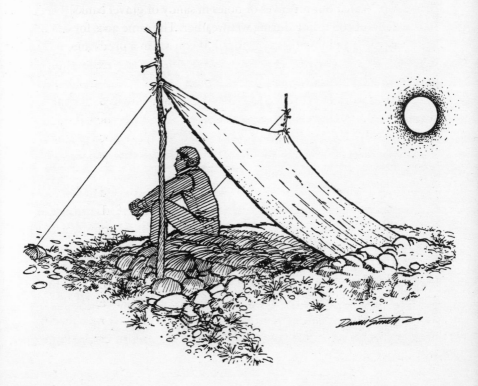

Fire Up

Searchers found the lost hiker in less than twenty-four hours. He was sitting against a large tree surrounded by the butts of about two packs of cigarettes and dozens of burned matches. He'd been dead for only a few hours.

This robust, healthy American lost his life under relatively mild weather conditions and while he had everything necessary to survive comfortably. Why?

He simply gave up, quit, stopped working at the business of living. The thought of being lost overwhelmed him, so he sat down and died.

Incredible? Yes, but it happens far too often.

Volumes have been written about the "will to live," the "positive mental attitude" and its importance in survival. One simple act does more for a survivor's peace of mind than any other—building a cheery fire.

Fire is useful to warm the body, but has other benefits too. Dancing flames warm the heart and cheer the soul. That's a big return from a simple oxidation process.

If the lost hiker had used one of his matches to start a fire, he would have found the fearful world around him far less menacing. It is hard to stay scared or depressed while you watch flames dance.

Ask any Boy or Girl Scout, "What are the elements necessary for a fire?" They will probably say, "Heat, fuel, and oxygen." That is simple enough. Anyone should be able to combine those elements and start a fire. You can too—if you really understand the chemical reaction involved.

For example; if you want to start a fire with a match and some half-inch twigs, what is your fuel? Careful! This is a trick question. The twigs are not really fuel. Fires burn gases, not solids or liquids. The things we call fuels burn only when they are heated enough to vaporize the combustible elements.

When you completely grasp that concept, fire building becomes easier. One match cannot heat half-inch sticks enough to vaporize them.

Let's take an easy-to-build fire and see how it works. Suppose you are on a day hike and want a fire to brew some afternoon tea. There's plenty of scrub brush and long-dead cactus along the trail. Your lunch is wrapped in waxed paper and you have a reliable cigarette lighter in your pocket.

Gather an armful of dead branches. Select a dry, level spot out of the wind and build your fire. You build the fire first—then you light it.

Crush the waxed paper into loose balls, and lay them on a flat rock or dry ground. Break some of the smallest twigs (1/8-inch or less) and stand them teepee fashion against the paper balls. Add some larger twigs (1/4-inch), taking care to leave space between them. These natural chimneys should be almost as wide as the sticks. Continue with your teepees until you have one-inch sticks all the way around, separated by appropriate chimney spaces.

Now, hold a flame under the paper balls. Since the tip of the flame is hottest, hold the lighter so the flame tip touches an exposed edge of the waxed paper. Within a minute you will have a blazing, relatively smokeless fire.

Okay, that was too easy, but demonstrates the principle. To produce fuel gases by vaporizing wood, you need either a big heat source or small wood. That is always true. If you want a survival fire, you will need a reliable source of intense heat, some very fine fuel material called tinder, and some sustaining "fuel." For ease of discussion, we will call the solid matter "fuel"—but remember, gases are the real fuel.

Arrange the tinder, kindling and fuel so each heats the other and adjacent pieces heat each other.

The best survival heat source is the pack of matches or lighter you carry with you. Forget about exotic stuff like rubbing sticks together, striking sparks from hard rocks, or concentrating the sun's heat with eye glasses or camera lenses. All of these methods will start a fire—but not under typical emergency conditions which would cause you to need a fire.

Tinder is the second ingredient in the fire chain. You will need it for every fire. It is often easiest to carry your own. Good tinder has lots of exposed surface area and a very thin cross section. You can use any substance that will magnify and sustain your original heat source until the larger fuel begins to vaporize.

In our example the waxed paper was an effective tinder, but we could have used dry desert flowers. Or perhaps have used a dollar bill if that's the only paper available.

With a heat source and some tinder in hand, it's time to look for some kindling. In order to vaporize heavier fuel, you will need some transition fuel to further magnify the heat of your tinder. Kindling can be twigs of pencil size, or slivers split from larger pieces of wood. It should be as dry as possible and graduated in size up to about one-inch in diameter.

Fuels for survival fires run the gamut from the obvious to the bizarre. We all tend to think about neat dry logs crackling into clean, orange flames—but even your spare tire may provide the smoking, stinking heat that saves your life. So it is best to let your imagination free-wheel a bit.

If you have the choice, nice dry hardwood makes the best fire. However, desert survivors usually can't be choosers, so use what you have. Just get plenty. Always gather more fuel than you think you could possibly need. You will be amazed at the prodigious appetite of even a small fire—and chances are in a survival situation you won't have a small fire. The tendency is to build a big comforting blaze, but....

Survival instructors quote an anonymous Native American who made fun of "White Man's Fires." "The Indian makes a small fire, sits close, stays warm. White man builds a big fire, sits back—and stays warm carrying more wood." Whoever he was, he was right. In a survival situation staying warm by carrying wood burns vital energy that you may not be able to replace. Let the fire work for you.

If wood is scarce in the spot your emergency chooses to happen, don't despair; there are other fuels and tinders. In desert-like areas dry sage and other brush burn very well. You can usually find enough for a small fire to get you through a cold night. Dry grass can be highly effective as both tinder and fuel for a survival fire.

If you are marooned with your vehicle, you can burn gasoline, motor oil, tires and floor mats. Gasoline is not an ideal fuel for open fires. In fact, it's downright dangerous; but if you really need a fire, gasoline is less dangerous than hypothermia. You should use caution, though.

If you have tools, you can disconnect a fuel line or drain the crankcase and collect the gasoline and oil in hub caps, rags, bottles, etc. Without tools it is more difficult, but you can still get at the gasoline. Use a knife or the jack handle to puncture the fuel tank. That may take some doing, but it is possible. Catch the gasoline and move it at least 25 feet crosswind from the car. If possible soak some sand, dry dirt or rags with the gasoline, then ignite it from the upwind side, using your free arm to shield your eyes and face. Expect a large flash before you get the match or lighter all the way to the gasoline. No external heat is required to vaporize gasoline, so the "fuel" is really floating around in the air near the liquid.

Never add more gasoline to a survival fire. If the fuel is running low in one fire, carry gasoline to a new spot several feet away crosswind, then carefully carry a burning bit of dirt or stick to the new gasoline supply, using the same precautions. Pouring gasoline into a fire is a sure way to get hurt!

Oil fires are built the same way, with saturated sand, etc. Or you can use motor oil as an assist for igniting wet wood. Motor oil is safe to work with and very effective.

Animal droppings make a useful fuel. Dry cattle or horse dung burns fairly well and is often found far from any other fuel. Frontiersmen learned to use "buffalo chips" to cook their coffee when nothing else was available.

Since we **build** fires, it seems logical that architecture should be important, and it is. By selecting the right architectural style you can insure a fast-starting, hot-burning fire every time. Get careless and that magic mix of heat, fuel and oxygen will go awry. The trick is to arrange the material so that each burning piece heats and supports the one next to it but lets air flow between.

Fire building is easy when conditions are ideal. When they are not, you must apply all the principles properly to get one going. ALWAYS, ALWAYS carry a fire starter when you are in the outdoors. The most versatile fire starters are lighters and matches. There are many commercial kits available, but those that provide both easy lighting and hot burning tinder are best.

Be sure the lighter or matches you carry will work when you need them. That means the lighter has to be reliable, preferably the butane type with a visible fuel supply. If you prefer matches, carry the strike-anywhere type in a waterproof container that you can open—even with cold, wet hands.

You can make tinder by filling a 35mm film can with cotton balls and soaking them with lighter fluid, then screwing the top on tightly and sealing with plastic tape. The saturated cotton will stay soaked for about a year when properly sealed and will burn for several minutes when placed at the base of a stack of other tinder and ignited. Candle stubs, jellied-petroleum products, wax-impregnated wood strips, fuel pellets, and fuel-soaked fiber are all excellent tinder. If you prefer going primitive, just carry a chunk of pitchwood or a piece of pitch in a little plastic bag.

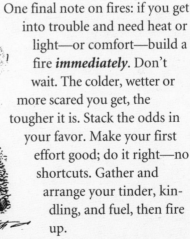

One final note on fires: if you get into trouble and need heat or light—or comfort—build a fire **immediately**. Don't wait. The colder, wetter or more scared you get, the tougher it is. Stack the odds in your favor. Make your first effort good; do it right—no shortcuts. Gather and arrange your tinder, kindling, and fuel, then fire up.

Make a Fuss

Alvin and Phyllis Oien and their daughter Carla found themselves marooned in the desert high country. The forced landing of their light plane had injured the Oiens, but not critically. Search planes flew almost six hundred hours over the area. Phyllis and Carla kept a diary while huddled in their plane—just eight miles from a U.S. highway for at least fifty-four days. Alvin had left after a few days to go for help. They were all extremely brave and courageous—but they all died. There was no evidence that they ever tried to signal the search planes which repeatedly flew overhead.

If you're in trouble and need help, you have to ask for it. You must tell the world. Even if you are a master of survival skills and capable of living off the land indefinitely, you still need to signal your fate and location to the outside world.

Signaling is not difficult. However, it does require some preparation or some on-the-spot ingenuity. Basically, all signals fall into three categories; visual, aural and electronic. Visual signals are designed to catch the eye of the searcher. They provide contrast in the form of color, shape or movement. The best ones employ all these. Aural signals are meant to emit sound that is louder and carries better than your own voice. They are designed for use when ground searchers are looking for you. Electronic signals are more sophisticated and more expensive than the other two but offer real advantages in range and versatility. They're worth the cost for some applications.

The ultimate goal of all signals is to make you stand out from your background. They do it by increasing contrast and range.

If you get lost while hunting, firing the traditional three shots into the air during the height of the shooting hours offers no contrast. Everyone is shooting then. Those same three shots fired after dark might get plenty of attention—at least from some alert game warden.

There are many effective and compact signals on the commercial market. Sporting goods stores, marinas, backpacking supply houses, and four-wheel drive centers are good places to look for them.

Flares of various types are the most popular signals. They come in day and night styles and have the advantage of convenience. On the other hand, they are one-shot signals; once you have fired a flare, it's gone. If you fail to draw attention to your predicament, you will have to use another flare or a different signal.

The better flares are self-igniting, usually by a pull-lanyard. Day flares emit dense clouds of red, orange or yellow smoke. They contrast well with almost any background and provide the additional eye-catcher of motion as the smoke billows out and catches the wind. Unfortunately, manufacturers can pack just so much smoke chemical into a reasonably small container.

Probably the king of flares is the old standard "day-night" model, made to military specifications and accepted by the Coast Guard. It is about the size of a stubby "D-Cell" flashlight and contains two flares which ignite when their respective lanyard is pulled. The "day" end emits a large orange smoke cloud that is visible for miles under good conditions. The "night" end burns with a blinding red flame that is almost impossible to miss. These flares are waterproof (in fact they will burn underwater) and very rugged. Try marine supply and diver's shops for them. Unbeaten for reliability, they are well worth the price.

Probably the least expensive flares are the common railroad fusee and highway flare. They are less than an inch in diameter and come in several lengths. These flares have a striker built into their red paper casing. Most auto accessory shops sell them. Highway flares have a bright red flame with a long burning time. They are best at night but bright enough to be fairly effective in daylight. You should not be without them.

Even a flat tire on a super highway can be a survival situation. A couple of flares spaced out behind your vehicle while you change the tire can save your life by diverting high-speed traffic.

Some of the other less expensive flares have a fuse or wick that must be lighted. They are not quite as weatherproof as the sealed, self-lighting styles; but they're okay as long as you remember to carry matches in a watertight case.

All flares share one limitation. They have to be used at the right moment—just before or just as the searcher looks in your direction.

Igniting a flare just after a search plane passes overhead is a disappointing waste.

The signal mirror is one of the most effective daytime signals. Mirror flashes have been seen from the air for over forty miles, and twenty-five miles is quite common. There are several styles and sizes of signal mirrors on the market, but they share common features. Each has a flat, reflective surface and some sort of sighting device which makes it easier to hit your target with the reflected flash.

Mirror flashes are most effective in relatively open terrain for ground-to-air signaling. However, they will also work for attracting the attention of ground searchers. Even on bright, overcast days you can use a mirror effectively.

Commercial signaling mirrors come with printed instructions telling you how to use the aiming device. But, any mirror or shiny object can become a signal mirror if you use the following method for sighting.

Face the mirror surface toward the sun and flash the reflected spot on a nearby object. Raise the mirror to your eye and reach out as far as you can with your free hand and "capture" the spot of light in the "V" formed by your extended thumb and fingers. Now turn your whole body and the mirror together, keeping the spotlight on the "V" until the target is also in the "V." The reflected sunspot will be right on target. Wobble the mirror very slightly to cause the spot to flash off and on. The combination of brilliant light and movement is hard to miss.

Even when no rescuer is in sight, practice scanning the horizon on surrounding hillsides with mirror flashes. Searchers can see your flashes farther than you can see the searcher.

Chemical lights can be used as survival signals. These fluid-filled tubes emit a ghostly green light after they are bent to fracture an inner vial of luminescent material. They're not extremely bright, but when combined with movement, they offer a convenient, unique signaling option.

Sound signals can be highly effective when there are ground searchers looking for you, or when you are trying to get your group back together. One of the best is the standard police whistle. Its high pitch and warbling effect (caused by the cork ball inside the whistle body) carries quite well and is far more durable than the human voice. When you're nervous or scared, your voice will wear out quickly.

Even better than whistles are the compressed gas-powered horns sold for athletic events and boats. These are fairly compact and, because of their lower pitch, carry farther than whistles. The smaller ones are compact enough to be practical for many outdoor uses.

Car or boat horns can be useful signals, too. A series of three blasts, repeated at regular intervals, will help searchers home in on your disabled rig. Firearms are okay, too, as long as you fire them at equally spaced intervals and at a time when someone is likely to notice.

Electronic devices may emit visual or aural signals. Strobe lights work much like the electronic flashes for cameras. When you switch on a survival strobe light, the battery charges a condenser which then discharges rapidly through a flash tube producing a blue-white flash. The process repeats automatically, about fifty times each minute until you shut off the switch or the battery dies. Strobes are extremely bright, but the duration of any single flash is very short. They don't offer quite the range of the better night flares, but they last a lot longer. Survival strobe lights are waterproof and rugged.

Other electronic devices include beacons, emergency locator transmitters (ELT) and two-way survival radios. These are special application devices. Beacons and ELT's transmit a beeping tone on the international radio distress frequency. They can be carried in a pocket or a pack and switched on manually in an emergency.

A young lady on a solo pack-train trip in California was rescued after severely injuring her back in a fall. An ELT signaled her emergency and led searchers to the rescue. However, beacons and ELT's are a bit expensive for wide application with the casual outdoorsman.

Still more expensive are two-way survival radios. They have been extremely successful in military combat rescues where exchange of information between survivor and rescuer may be vital, but their cost argues against use by the general public.

Widely available signaling devices are the Citizen Band Radio and the mobile cellular telephone. Channel 9, the CB emergency frequency, is monitored by volunteers in many areas so your emergency transmission has a good chance of being picked up, or a 911 call on a mobile phone could be the solution to your survival situation. If you are in an isolated spot and don't make contact, try to move your CB or phone to the highest point in the area.

Before exhausting your battery, gather the best information you have available on your location. A Global Positioning System (GPS) can be very helpful in this situation, but don't overlook the road maps in your glove compartment to come up with a good estimate.

But, suppose you need help and have no signals. No need to despair. You can improvise effective signals. We've already looked at one—the improvised signal mirror.

The fire you build for reassurance or warmth can be a good signal, too. Simply make sure that it contrasts well. It should be highly visible and must be different from other campfires in the area. Remember, a search plane pilot may fly over hundreds of square miles looking for you, and there could be dozens of other fires to distract him.

One way to stand out is to build three signal fires, set at the corners of a large triangle, about 150 feet apart. That's an international distress signal. Keep the fires bright at night and smoky during the day. If a triangle is impractical, use a straight line. The key is to make your fires different—and a set of three fires in a geometric pattern is very unnatural. It will get attention.

Another way to get attention is to make your smoke a different color. Most burning wood produces white smoke—so make yours black. You can make black smoke by burning oil from your car, boat, plane or cycle engine. Tires, fan belts, radiator hoses, or boot heels work, too.

You can also create contrast for yourself by using shadows and geometrical shapes. Straight lines are uncommon in nature, so anything you can build with them will be noticeable from the air—such as rocks laid out in a long line or logs laid end to end. If you orient your line so the sun will cast shadows on one side of your line, so much the better.

Moving signals work! A hiker was rescued because he tied two red plastic jugs to long poles, then spun the poles to fling the jugs in a wild arc.

Remember, when you're in trouble, don't sit there and stew about it. Make a fuss. A BIG FUSS!

First Things First

Life is a matter of setting priorities. Each day we make decisions on how to use our time, spend our money, please our boss—or family—or friends. We unconsciously rank-order virtually everything we do from "absolutely essential" to "ho-hum." The list is constantly changing.

On Monday morning, excelling on the job or in class or trying some great new recipe may be right up there near the top. By Friday noon that spot is probably occupied by planning or dreaming of some weekend activity.

Survival is no different from everyday life. It's still a matter of setting priorities—but the stakes are higher, and the feedback is quicker.

A young boy and his dad were exploring in the Mojave Desert on a hot Saturday morning. After a vigorous hike and checking out some old mines, they returned to their pick-up and got stuck trying to turn around in loose sand.

Until that moment they had only been interested in the mystique and nostalgia of desert ruins. Now their only thought was to get their truck out of the sand. They dug furiously around the mired wheels, tried to jack up the rear end, built ramps ahead of the tires—and worked up a soaking sweat. Finally, in utter frustration, they struck out on foot. They never made it. Searchers found their bodies the next day, less than a mile from a main highway.

The official cause of death was dehydration, but what really caused that pleasant outing to end in tragedy? They set the wrong priorities. The overwhelming desire to get home probably causes more problems for survivors than any other single thing. Pilots call it "get-home-itis."

There are no pat answers in survival. But let's Monday-morning quarterback this typical desert problem and see what it can teach us.

Father and son were probably disgusted with themselves for getting stuck. That's a common survivor reaction. You can expect to feel guilty and blame yourself when you get into a survival situation. But if you let that feeling drive you to mix up your priorities, you can get into real trouble.

Because these survivors wanted to get home, they exerted themselves in the harsh desert heat and lost precious body water through excess perspiration. When their first attempts failed, they merely redoubled their efforts to get out. Trying to walk out in the midday heat without canteens was foolhardy—but walking *away* from the thirty gallons of water in their camper was incredible!

When they got stuck, there was really no immediate problem. About the only hazard they faced was the hot desert sun. Attempting to dig the pickup out of the sand by building gently sloping ramps in front of the wheels and lining them with floor mats was good procedure too. But their problems began when freeing the truck became their number one priority. The hazard was heat, but they apparently thought being immobile was more pressing. When they should have been protecting their bodies from heat and dehydration, they put all their reserve of energy, body water, and brain power into getting unstuck.

Probably all of us would have initially tried to get the vehicle out of the sand. That's fine—*if* you work slowly, carefully and avoid sweating too much. Also, if you have water, use it to keep your electrolytes in balance. If the cause begins to look hopeless, or you get fatigued, *quit*. Sit in the *shade* and rest.

If the two weary explorers had just given up before they were exhausted, taken a big drink of water, and sat in the shade until sunset, they could have walked to the highway with ease.

Normally, your number one priority in a survival situation is to protect your body.

Once you have the body protection problem solved, it's time to think about getting home. Survival is *not* living off the land indefinitely. It is getting back home as quickly and as comfortably as possible. Your goal should be to make any survival situation as easy and as short as possible.

Strange as it may seem, one of the biggest hurdles faced by survivors is making the decision to *actively* try to get rescued.

Your next priority should be to sustain or maintain your body. One of the best ways to insure that you give yourself the chance to survive an emergency is to keep fully hydrated. It takes between two and four quarts of liquids each day to keep you at peak efficiency—even if you avoid strenuous exercise!

Naturally, we get a large portion of that in or with our food, but we still have to drink a lot of water or beverages to stay at our peak. As explained in Chapter 2, the early symptoms of dehydration are vague and sneaky. Unless you are in the habit of drinking a lot of water, regardless of your activity, it is highly probable that your efficiency is marred by some lack of body water.

If an emergency strikes and your access to water is cut off, you will go downhill rapidly. The best way to prevent survival water problems is to keep your tanks full at *all* times. If you begin an emergency fully hydrated, you can expect to survive for about five days without additional water—even at 100 degrees in the shade. Don't prejudice your fun or your survival potential by going around with half a tank of water.

Food is far less critical than water. You can expect to survive for several weeks on nothing more than the food stored in your body. You will not be comfortable and you will lose a lot of energy, but the body machine will still function.

A Special Precaution

This can be more important to you and those who care about you than any of the survival priorities. It is one you can practice without ever having a personal emergency. Pilots call it filing a flight plan.

Always tell someone where you are going and when you'll be back. That sounds easy, but most people just go.

However, unless someone knows where you are and how long you plan to be there, any emergency can be a long and lonely one. More on this in Chapter 7.

You can survive virtually any emergency if you know the basics, keep your head—and put first things first.

Rescue and You

Rescue is not a one-way street. When you're in trouble, it makes no more sense to simply sit down and wait to be found than to run around aimlessly in blind panic. Teamwork really pays off in a search and rescue mission—and you are part of the team! You need to know the other players.

Search and rescue (SAR) agencies have two distinct and separate functions. First, they are geared to rescue people in emergencies. Rescue requires fast action but relatively few people. However, they must be well trained to handle injuries, transportation, mountain climbing, emergency cutting tools for entering wrecked vehicles, and many other skills. These are the heroes of books and popular television shows. Their jobs are difficult, dangerous and highly visible.

The other side of the SAR coin is search—far more mundane and frustrating. But without effective search operations, the rescue people would have few pickups to make. Searches often involve hundreds of people with varying amounts of training. This side of SAR isn't as glamorous, but it is extremely important to you. Until you are found, you have no chance of being rescued.

SAR coordinators know that the first six hours of any search are the most critical. People without survival knowledge will often get themselves into such a predicament by then, that rescue is far less likely. As a result, SAR folks pull out all the stops to locate you *fast*. That means you have to start thinking about making contact with them as soon as you think you will be missed.

Your odds are a lot better if you understand the search problem. The old stereotype of hundreds of people, shoulder to shoulder, marching through the desert is an unsophisticated last-ditch effort today. It is far more likely the coordinators of your search will try to out-guess you. They will attempt to figure out what happened to you and what you are likely to do about it. With the specifics of thousands of searches stored in computer memory, they can call up similar situations, based on weather, terrain, age, experience, etc.

Analysis of that data provides a pretty good idea of where to concentrate the effort to create the best odds of finding you within six hours. It's a numbers game. The coordinator has just so many people and so much time. He may have hundreds of square miles to cover, so he has to play the odds. Fortunately, it works—most of the time.

When you are in trouble and need help, take care of yourself and remember, someone is trying to figure out where you are and what you'll do. Whenever practical, stay close to your vehicle, boat or aircraft. Searchers will almost always find your vehicle first.

You and the searchers have responsibilities to each other. You can both reasonably expect certain things of the other. According to Rick Lavalla, former President of the National Association of Search and Rescue (NASAR), you can expect them to:

Respond Fast	Once they know you are missing.
Confine the Search Area	Based on what likely happened to you and what you're apt to do.
Search at Night	That's right; they'll be out there, so don't completely hole up. You can be easier to find at night—but not if you are sacked out in a shelter made of natural materials and have no fire.
Search for Clues	If you must move, try to leave notes, bits of clothing, blaze marks or arrows on the ground to mark your direction of travel.
Search with a Plan and Organization	Don't foul them up by being rash and unorganized in *your* actions.
Use a Grid Search as a Last Resort	This is the classic shoulder-to-shoulder sweep of an entire area. When they use it, all else has failed; but it does work. Grid search is especially effective for disabled survivors or very frightened children.

The first, hasty search will be run with horses, vehicles, airplanes or on foot right through the center of the probable search area. They will use roads, trails or streams to speed this step; and they will be looking for clues, signals or other evidence that will narrow the search.

If the hasty search turns up some leads, the coordinators may put trackers on your trail. You can expect Indian-style trackers, trained to follow the marks you leave on the terrain or dogs trained to follow your scent. They may even use dogs that search in a set pattern, depending upon all their senses to locate you. In either case, success is high. That means quicker rescue for you and less demand on man-power for the coordinator.

You can expect searchers to use a wide variety of vehicles. Helicopters and fixed-wing aircraft may be called into service. Four-wheel drive rigs may patrol roads and trails, horses may be used cross-country, but your chances of quick rescue will improve dramatically if you can get on or near some place vehicles can travel.

One thought to remember—if your emergency was caused by weather conditions that stalled your vehicle, searchers will probably have no better luck with similar vehicles.

SAR programs vary from state to state. Usually the county sheriff or the state police will have the prime responsibility to find you on private, national forest, or Bureau of Land Management land. If you are in a national park, the ranger usually has the task of locating and rescuing you. The U.S. Coast Guard has prime responsibility for searching on large inland lakes.

Many states have departments of emergency services (or some similarly named organizations) which assist local agencies in coordinating SAR efforts and in training SAR teams. Some states have full-time public awareness, training, and integrated SAR resources. If you get into trouble in these states, you can expect a top-notch, smoothly run operation with no wasted motions.

Regardless of who is in charge, you can bet they will have a host of agencies eager and able to assist. The coordinator may call upon desert rescue teams, four-wheel drive clubs, law enforcement agencies, explorer search and rescue units, fire departments, military organizations and CB radio REACT units—to name a few.

Many of the people involved in search and rescue operations are volunteers. Often they risk their personal vehicles and their necks to find you and bring you home. The state may pick up part of their gas bill, but most are volunteers in the purest sense. Their dedication warrants a simple action on your part, so let's look at *your* role on the SAR team.

File a Flight Plan

First, and foremost, *always* leave a "flight plan" with a responsible person. Tell *where* you are going, *how many* in your party, *what* they are wearing and carrying, and *when* you will be back. Include your vehicle license number and expected parking spot; tell them to notify the authorities if you don't call within a specified "grace period" after your expected return. You can set the grace period to suit the difficulty of your outdoor event and your promptness. If you're the type who is always a half-hour late, don't tell them to cry wolf when you're only an hour overdue.

Suppose you leave work at 4:30 on a sunny afternoon and decide to detour through the beautiful desert on the way home. It is a spur-of-the-moment decision and no one else knows what you have in mind. The utter peace and beauty of the spot is just too much after a hard day at work, so you decide to take a walk. Parking the car near the road on an intriguing trail, you stride along the path, savoring the sights and smells of nature at her best.

A pretty picture, isn't it? But what happens if you slip and wrench your back and the pain is too severe to let you walk the mile or so back to the car? You will probably be missed when you fail to show up for supper, or a date, or for work the next morning. Then what? Certainly, no one is going to start searching the desert for you—at least not right away.

Probably someone will begin to worry and begin a telephone search for you among friends and relatives. When that turns up nothing, they may call the police, who will begin to look for your car. Someone will suspect foul play. County or state authorities will probably start looking for your car in more out-of-the-way places. Eventually, they'll probably find it and start searching for you.

All of that activity takes time. Everyone is operating in the dark. There are thousands of miles of roads to cover and hundreds of square miles where you might be—and there's no hint of where to start. While the world gears up to look for you, that back is going to hurt like blazes and you're going to be angry at yourself and everything in general for your predicament.

One quick phone call—from a roadside booth or car phone—could have avoided it all. If you had told your roommate, spouse, close friend or co-worker that you were going to drive down "old 99" for a look at the desert, your chances of spending a painful night out there would be almost nil. If you failed to return at the appointed time, a more directed search could be instigated. With only one route to search, the police would find the car and you in minutes rather than hours or days.

There *is* a tougher problem. It can be incredibly hard to follow your "flight plan." It seems there is always one more ridge to cross, one more trail to check out, or another ghost town to explore. Something always beckons you to leave your pre-announced spot for one that looks better. That almost overwhelming urge to "see what's over the hill" can be tough to control, but if you get into trouble, you will be glad you are where you said you would be.

One way to avoid iron-clad restrictions and still be in a position for quick help if trouble arises is to leave a "change of flight plan" in a conspicuous spot. Put a note on the dashboard of your car or some other obvious place before you leave for a new destination. Give your new plan, your time of departure, and estimated return. If you are

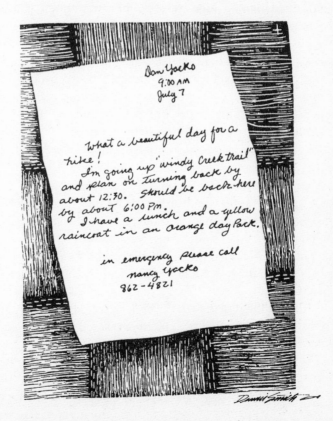

going to park a long distance from your planned spot, it might be worth making a phone call from a roadside booth.

Jennifer was an avid amateur wildlife photographer from the Midwest. She was eager to add some shots of desert animals to her collection. She told the desk clerk at her motel where she'd park her car, the general direction she would walk in, and that she expected to be back shortly after sunset. After parking the car on a seldom-used dirt road, Jennifer tore open a film box and scrawled on it, "GOING NORTHEAST," and dropped it on the seat.

A mile or so down the trail, she startled a desert bighorn and almost got his picture at thirty yards. Time after time that cagey ram let her get almost within good photo range and then dashed over the next ridge. Jennifer was able to get a lot of quick shots of his backside, but nothing like what she wanted. She noted that the sheep was angling back toward the road near her car. He crossed within sight of her parking spot.

After two hours of hide and seek, there was no way Jennifer was going to give up the chase in spite of the fact that she was now going in the opposite direction indicated by her note. But she was still thinking. Just after crossing the road she laid a bright yellow film box on a con-spicuous rock. Finally, the old ram stopped to look back. This time he was posed on a small cliff with the setting sun illuminating his massive horns. At the click of the shutter, he bolted, but stopped a few yards away.

Jennifer made a quick step—caught her boot between two rocks and fell sideways. The pain in her ankle almost caused her to black out. She was disabled a long way from her "flight plan" location.

About two hours after sunset, the desk clerk called the county sheriff, saying Jennifer was overdue. He set up a hasty search of the roads and trails and soon located the car. Two searchers walked north-east, based on Jennifer's note, but several walked along the road with flashlights. They spotted the film box, recalled the foot searchers and headed into the canyon. An hour later Jennifer was riding to the hospital in a patrol car.

By filing a flight plan with the desk clerk and keeping it up to date with the note and the film box, Jennifer insured her own rescue. You can do the same.

Do Not Go Alone

Jennifer would have been far better off if she'd taken a friend on her photo trek. We all like to be alone occasionally, and the desert is a great place to meditate or unwind—but is unforgiving when you get hurt, sick or lost. You can avoid many hazards by merely having a partner.

Take Proper Equipment

Your prime responsibility in your own rescue is to take care of your body until someone can rescue it. So why not make it easy? Dress for the activity and carry clothes for the environment en route (see "What to Wear," Chapter 9). Carry some selected equipment, especially WATER (see "What to Carry," Chapter 10). Perhaps the most crucial preparation of all is to make sure you are properly equipped *inside*. Start your trip with a "full tank" of rest, water and nourishing foods. A lot of people get into trouble because they wear themselves down or use up their reserves just getting to their jumping off point. Driving all night, drinking only coffee (or, worse yet, alcohol), skipping breakfast, or launching a tough trip when you are simply out of shape is inviting trouble.

Let Them Find You

Strange as it may seem, there is a good chance you are going to have a tendency to *avoid* your rescuers. That is one of the problems facing search teams everywhere. It seems to be some sort of ego reaction. All of us feel some reluctance to admit mistakes—especially when they cause other people inconvenience, money or personal risk.

Imagine your thoughts if you were stranded due to your error in judgment. Maybe you misjudged the weather, or trusted the old fan belts on your car a bit too much. You are not hurt and you know dozens of people are out there in the middle of the night looking for you. That is a tough nut for anyone's ego to accept. Are you going to swallow your pride and make every effort to contact the searchers? Or will you hide in embarrassment and hope to sneak out behind them?

Don't be too quick to answer that one. It's better to simply accept yourself as human, prone to make mistakes and reluctant to broadcast those which impact on others—especially when you are under stress. The tendency to cover up will be there, so why not admit it and decide right now that you will *help your rescuers find you.*

Think how pleased and proud they will be to conclude a well-planned and organized search. They'll be happy and you will be comfortable.

Stay Put

Survivors have a strong urge to move. Maybe we have all read too many stories and seen too many movies of people "walking out" through incredible hardships. The traditional cartoon of the gaunt, bearded survivor crawling through the desert has become an American classic. Now is the time to recognize the very human desire to move when confronted with discomfort, fear or embarrassment. And now is the time to convince yourself to stay put.

A light plane crashed in rugged desert near Las Vegas. The pilot was killed. His passenger, who suffered a head injury, wandered away from the crash site, and eventually sought shelter under some thick brush. Over a hundred ground searchers and several aircraft combed the mountainsides and found the downed plane with its pilot in a matter of hours. Bad weather hampered further searching, but the SAR force stayed on the job. They found the passenger, too—28 days later! He was dead by then, and we'll never know whether his head injury clouded his judgment or whether he merely succumbed to the desire to move away from unpleasant surroundings. One thing is sure. If he'd stayed with the plane, he would have been found almost a month earlier.

There are several reasons you should stay put in a survival situation. If you're within a vehicle, you are a bigger target for searchers. Also, there are limits to where any vehicle can go. When the SAR coordinator knows what kind of vehicle you have, he may be able to eliminate 90 percent of the search area and concentrate his people on where you are most apt to be—if you stay with or near the vehicle.

When you are lost on foot there are other reasons to make yourself comfortable and stay where you are. Trying to walk out can get you hurt, especially when you are anxious and distressed. You are not going to be concentrating on how and where you walk. One missed step can compound your problem.

There's also a good possibility you may walk right out of the primary search area. No search can cover the whole desert. If you wander into country that is not being searched *intensively*, there is far less chance you will be found. Finally, the SAR coordinator is using every device of technology and experience to *predict* where you are. Do not foul him up by wandering into some remote canyon.

In a survival situation you may need all the energy and water you have, so don't waste energy walking unless you *know* exactly where you are going, *know* how to get there, and *know* you can make it without exhausting yourself. If you do walk, leave a trail. "Tell" the searchers where you have gone. Leave a note or bits of clothing along your route.

Get Involved

When you are in trouble and need help, it's *your* rescue that counts. So take part in it! Do everything you can to be found by signaling to anything that moves. Reread "Make a Fuss," Chapter 5, and by all means make one!

You can count on the SAR folks to perform their role very professionally. If you do your part, any survival situation you experience will be a short one. The only better one is the one that doesn't happen.

Water in the Desert

Even if you carefully keep yourself hydrated, a desert emergency in hot weather will rob you of body water quickly and require a refill. The *only* dependable way to replenish your body water in the desert is by *carrying* it with you at all times and in quantity. There is more about that in Chapter 10.

If you run out or lose your supply, it is possible to get water in the desert. Possible does not mean easy! Any water you get from the desert is going to demand payment in sweat and lost energy. You have to constantly balance the cost against the benefit. For example, you might dig down six feet in a sandy, dry creek bed and get a quart of water a day seeping into the hole. You may have lost a gallon of water in sweat digging the hole. There is very little free water in the desert.

However, there are three ways of getting what is there. You can find it, catch it or "make" it.

Finding Water

Finding water in most desert areas requires careful observation. If you are lucky enough to have your desert emergency near a reservoir, stock tank or operating windmill, you may have all the water you could need at little cost in sweat. If you know one of those sources is ten miles away, across a 3,000 foot ridge, it might cost too much sweat to get to it. Watch for stock tanks or windmills by observing cattle or game animals early in the morning or late in the evening. They will go to water then, and you may be able to follow. Obviously, if you see buildings, it's wise to check them out, too.

Sometimes you can find good water in abundance, even in the most parched landscape—if you are really observant.

Greg was with a party of hikers in the Grand Canyon. Their leader had badly underestimated the amount of water they would need. As they climbed the 3,000 feet out of the canyon, all of them suffered from dehydration, and their canteens were dry. Several of the hikers were stumbling and falling. The sun, beating against the north rim, sapped their strength.

Greg was hurting too, but he was alert. Everyone had quit talking. In the quiet he thought he heard water running. After first brushing it off as his imagination, he went to investigate—and found a huge spring. The rest of the climb was a piece of cake.

Not all springs are so spectacular, but even small seeps can provide water to a survivor. They will usually be marked by relatively lush green vegetation. When the spring has stopped flowing or is barely seeping water, you may be able to encourage it by digging just below the wettest, greenest spot. If there is any significant moisture, you may be able to mop it up with a piece of cloth and wring it into a container.

Depressions in desert rock formations sometimes trap and hold rain water for quite a while. You may be alerted to these puddles by regular activity of birds or animals, or by swarms of insects hovering above them.

If you're lucky enough to find surface water, it should be purified by boiling for ten minutes or with water purification tablets.

Catching Water

All deserts get rain. If you see clouds building up, get ready to catch any rain that falls. Ponchos, raincoats, and plastic sheets or bags will catch and direct rain water to a container. Stretch them out to expose the most surface to the shower and angle them so you can catch all the water that hits them. Use extra clothing to soak up rain also, but be careful. It would accomplish little to soak all your clothes in an afternoon thundershower only to become hypothermic during the cold desert night.

Those nights often produce dew, and you may be able to catch some by wiping it from cool surfaces with cloth early in the morning. It's possible to collect dew by laying plastic or a poncho in a small depression in the ground.

Some dry desert stream beds have saturated soil below the surface. The best place to dig is against the outside bank on a sharp bend. Water may be close to the surface or very deep. Any wet soil you hit may produce some water, but digging is a powerful sweat stealer.

Barrel cacti are a usable source of water. However, they are hard to open without getting hurt. Cut or chop off the top of the cactus and use a stick to mash the inner pulp. If the resulting juice is milky, find another cactus. If it is clear, use the edibility test in Chapter 11 to verify its potability. You may have to wrap the pulp in cloth and wring the water out. There are too many varieties of cactus and too many possible conditions for general rules about the quality of water they contain.

"Making Water"

There is water in the driest desert, in the air, in the soil, and in the plants. Another means of tapping it is a homemade still. Three common types are relatively easy to use. All use heat to evaporate water from soil, plants or contaminated liquid and a cooler surface to condense and collect it.

The solar still is made by digging a hole about three feet across and two feet deep in the moistest soil you find. Place a container to collect the water at the bottom. Line the hole with vegetation or wet it with contaminated water (the water in your vehicle's radiator). Cover it with a sheet of clear plastic, secure the edge with dirt and place a small, smooth stone in the center to provide a cone with approximately 30-degree sides. Sun shining through the plastic will evaporate water from the soil and the vegetation, and you will see it condensing on the plastic in about an hour. Water production is not spectacular—about a cupful per eight hours of direct sun in good conditions. It will take several stills to sustain you, and constructing each one will cost sweat.

Another method is the vegetation-bag still. To make one, fill a large, clear plastic bag with green vegetation or crushed cactus and secure the top. Lay the bag so that water cannot run directly from the vegetation to the corners of the bag. You want the condensed droplets to run down off the top surface of the bag and into the reservoir corner. Production is somewhat better than the solar still, and you should expend less sweat building the vegetation still. The water may be like a bitter tea, due to the heating and steeping of the vegetation. It can pick up plant toxins. Be safe by using the edibility test.

Easier to make and a better producer is the transpiration still. All plants take water from the soil and transpire it into the air, much like you sweat. You can trap this water by tying a clear plastic bag over a cluster of living branches. Tie the bag closed around the branches and tie it down so a corner catches the condensed droplets. If there are any green plants around, you can set up several of these in an hour without undue sweating. Production depends on the plant and sub-soil moisture, but it can be impressive. In one test, a single bag produced about a gallon per day for three days, on the same branch. That's worth the sweat!

A final word. Do not depend on *getting* water in the desert. *Carry* it.

9

What to Wear

It was a beautiful afternoon. Every bend in the trail brought new sights and fresh scents of wild flowers. A bright March sun warmed the high desert to nearly sixty degrees. No clouds marred the cobalt blue sky, and there was not a hint of a breeze. Little wonder the two hikers had set off in shorts and cotton sweat shirts. Their steady climb was more than enough to keep them warm and comfortable. Even during their frequent pauses to soak up the color and majesty of high desert springtime, they did not get chilled.

About two o'clock a light wind began to blow from the nearby mountains. It was a bit chilly, but picking up their pace still kept Michael and Judy warm. Within fifteen minutes the sun was blotted out by thick, gray clouds, and a few drops of rain tickled their cheeks. Michael estimated they were about five miles up the trail, so they elected to continue, rather than return to their Volkswagen.

They noted the change in aroma from the desert plants, and Michael commented on its freshness. "What a relief after breathing smog all week. I always love that delicious scent in the air just before a rain, and up here it's even better." Before they could get their rain jackets out of their day packs, it was raining hard. They donned the colorful yellow and blue nylon shells over slightly soggy sweatshirts, and hurried on toward the cabin. Their momentary chill evaporated in the first 100 hundred yards of gentle climbing.

In spite of a rising wind and dropping temperature, it came as a complete surprise when Michael started shivering during their next rest break. But he laughed it off, "Guess I should have put on my rubber boots to play in the rain." Judy didn't feel the cold yet, but she was concerned. "Come on, Michael. Let's hurry and get under cover. We don't want you sick tomorrow."

About a mile from the shack—and several hundred feet below it, they stopped to rest again. Michael was shaking uncontrollably and his speech was slurred. "Michael, quit kidding. You sound like a drunk." Judy tried to sound casual, but she was shivering too. Michael stumbled and fell twice in the first 200 yards after the break. The second time he had trouble getting up. He was becoming dangerously hypothermic.

This typical episode had a happy ending. Michael was assisted by hikers that Judy signaled. He took a lot of good natured kidding, but both he and Judy learned something about clothing.

Your first defense against hypothermia and hyperthermia is the clothes you wear. Judy and Michael found that wet cotton gave practically no protection (90 percent less than dry cotton). It would be great if we could all go about our favorite outdoor activity dressed for protection from Death Valley heat to New Mexico highlands. Even if we could approach this kind of protection, none of us would wear the required space-age suit. Let's face it, most of us are far more interested in how we look than in survival preparedness. That's fine, but it is no reason to forget completely that those stylish duds might have to protect your vulnerable body.

You'll just have to strive for a blend of style, comfort and protection. It *can be* done! Let's take a look at some typical outdoor activities and see how it works.

Hiking, Backpacking and Riding

If Michael and Judy had altered their gear just a little they could have both easily concluded their hike without assistance.

On any hike or ride, even in the desert, it's wise to expect rain and wind. Desert showers come up fast, and they can rob you of body heat, even when the air temperature never gets much below that in your living room. How long would you stay warm while you were wet and nude in a sixty-five degree room with a fan blowing on you? A layer or two of wet cotton will not provide much more protection than that, and synthetics are even worse.

Wool is the classic fabric of the outdoorsman. For centuries some cultures have endured harsh environments with no protection other than wool. Desert-dwelling Bedouins wear it year-round. This natural miracle fabric has some unique properties. It generally has a lot of insulating dead air space between its fibers. It retains much of its insulating value even when wet. Finally, it tends to shed water because of its lanolin content.

If Michael and Judy had just replaced their cotton sweatshirts with loosely knit wool sweaters, they would have been just as comfortable during their hike. Yet their rests would not have been chilling. When they donned their windproof rain jackets, the air trapped in those sweaters (with no wind to disturb it) would have provided excellent insulation.

The most fashion-conscious hiker will have to admit that a colorful wool sweater is at least as good looking as a cotton shirt or sweatshirt. By combining a wool sweater or shirt with a wind-rain jacket and a wool stocking cap, you have taken care of almost any summer threat to your upper half. Why the cap? Because you can lose about three-fourths of all the heat your body can produce through your unprotected head.

Shorts are fine for hiking or light climbing in moderate temperatures and open country, but they leave a lot of leg exposed to lose heat in a cool-wet environment. One of the easiest ways to overcome this limitation is to carry a light pair of wool trousers in your day pack. When the weather turns sour, just stop and pull them on over the shorts.

The cleverest solution I have seen to the shorts problem was conceived by a sharp Colorado woman. Gail made her hiking shorts out of a pair of soft wool trousers. She cut off the legs and installed a round-the-leg zipper on each. A one-inch flap of material extended below the zipper on each leg of the shorts to protect her thighs from the zipper teeth. She carried the pant legs in her day pack. Within seconds those shorts could be converted into warm survival pants.

Another possibility is to carry a lightweight raincoat and a pair of nylon rainpants in your pack. Neither are quite as good as wool pants, but they will stop the cold desert wind and keep you dry if you get caught in a shower.

In hot weather there is a strong tendency to strip down, but don't do it. Proper clothing is your best protection from heat and dehydration. The desert sun can be brutal. Direct and reflected ultra-violet rays can burn your skin in minutes. Lightweight, white, loose-fitting, long-sleeved shirts and long pants are your best bet. They will reflect much of the sun's heat and protect your skin. Other light colors also offer good protection, but white clothes have the added advantage of making you easier for searchers to spot if you should get hurt and are unable to signal.

Be sure to include a wide-brimmed hat to protect your head and neck. Straw hats are coolest in the hot sun, yet do a fair job of keeping your head warm on cold nights. A large neckerchief is valuable to hang down your neck, French Foreign Legion style, to give even more protection. Make it a bright colored one and you have a fine signal as well (see Chapter 5).

Protecting your feet in the desert is vital. Sharp rocks and spiny plants will try to impale them, while searing surface temperatures bake them. Wear sturdy leather boots with thick, rugged soles and at least two pair of socks. Carry extra socks (see Chapter 10) so you can change frequently to prevent blisters. Dry the damp ones immediately, so they will be ready to use again.

DENNIS SMITH

Driving

People do not tend to dress to drive, let alone dress to survive. They usually dress to arrive. If your destination is a business meeting or a luncheon, you probably wear a business suit or casual dress. You wear sports clothes and shoes to a picnic, formal attire to a concert. The point is, you rarely think about the environment you travel through. You may cross a high mountain pass on the way to that picnic, but it does not register as subarctic. Shorts and a tee-shirt will offer little protection from the scorching desert between Indio and Blythe.

Instead of trying to match clothes to the multi-faceted environments a car or four-wheel-drive rig will take you through, simply toss some extra clothes into a box, suitcase or plastic bag in the trunk.

Suppose you live in San Bernardino and you regularly drive within a 200-mile radius of there. Within two hours you can be in desert heat of 120 degrees or face a snow squall in the mountain passes. By putting an old hat, an out-of-style coat and a pair of sturdy shoes or boots into the trunk for each passenger and keeping a couple of pairs of sunglasses in the glove compartment, you can set out for any destination in the area in any clothes that seem appropriate without being concerned about a breakdown. Also, an old umbrella makes a great sunshade.

Flying

If you fly your own plane regularly, you have a special survival problem. The speed and freedom of your magic carpet take you over a wide variety of environments, and it is next to impossible to dress for them all. Also, the warmth and comfort of the cockpit tend to make us forget just how miserable we might be after an unplanned landing.

Suppose you are planning a September trip from West Texas to Southern California. You may fly over semi-desert sandhills, high plains, mountains, some true desert and finally horizon-to-horizon city. If you have to land unexpectedly en route, you could be uncomfortable.

Diversity of environmental problems complicates the "What to Wear" problem for pilots and passengers in light aircraft. Fortunately, there are some ways to cope with it. One of the easiest answers is to wear a flying suit like military pilots do. The utter utility of multi-pocketed coveralls is hard to beat.

With a good quality flight suit as an outer layer, even a business suit becomes an acceptable survival garment for moderate temperatures. If you fly over really cold areas, carry a set of the quilted type of insulated underwear. They weigh very little and offer super protection.

In really hot weather the suit will protect you from the sun and scorching rocks or sand. Try to find one that has side zippers, as well as the one in front. They allow you to ventilate the suit better.

With a flying suit, insulated underwear, and a good hat, you are nearly prepared for a survival situation, but you will need boots. This is the only clothing item that's really a weight problem. If pounds are critical in your aircraft, I would recommend wearing boots instead of shoes when you fly. That way the additional weight is insignificant. There are sturdy boots available that are dressy enough to wear with a business suit. Western pilots often wear cowboy boots with almost anything. They are not bad as survival protection either. If you have room to stow a pair of boots, it is probably better to get a pair of lug-soled, lace-up boots about eight inches high and stuff them with extra wool socks before you pack them into the aircraft.

Don't forget your passengers. Remember that they are your responsibility. A few extra clothing items may make a big difference.

Whatever your favorite outdoor activity, remember the clothes on your back are your first line of defense in an emergency. Give them some thought. Use these examples—and some ingenuity—and develop a wardrobe for your sport and your area. Merely wearing the right clothing can turn a potentially serious event into a "piece of cake."

What to Carry

Larry and Jean were hiking in the Southern California desert. They underestimated the harsh drying effects of low humidity, temperatures in the nineties, and climbing back out of a steep canyon. By the time they slumped in the shade of their four-wheel drive rig, they were feeling sick, and Larry had a throbbing headache. They were dehydrated. Both drank heavily from the big canteen behind the front seat, but the water really didn't help much. Jean suspected that Larry had lost too much salt during his sweaty climb. She broke open their vehicle survival kit and gave him a can of slightly salty, sun-warmed beef vegetable soup. Larry told me he could almost feel that salt going into his bloodstream. They both finished the day as actively and enthusiastically as they had begun it. There was no survival episode this time, but the survival kit made the difference.

Survival kits do not need to be expensive, bulky or heavy. They do need to be tailored to your activity, your needs, and the weather in your area; the kit should be convenient to keep with you so it is available when you need it. Even the most minimal kit can save the day.

Your own kit should be easy to carry—so you'll **always** carry it when you are away from civilization. It should contain the basics to allow you to create a life-support system. It should provide some means of attracting attention. It need not be complicated, and you can do it yourself. There is no reason to buy an expensive, commercial survival kit. In fact, a homemade kit has some very real advantages over even the best-designed commercial one. It can be tailored to *your* needs, *your* sports and *your* area. Even more important, you will know each item and why you included it. That is far better than breaking open a store-bought kit during an emergency and being surprised by what is inside—or what is *not*.

Start with a container. That may sound backwards, and you may prefer to assemble your components, then search for something that will hold them. However, the activity frequently dictates the maximum size and weight of the kit, so I prefer to start with a convenient container. After all, the goal is a kit you will *always* carry, not an exotic stay-at-home one.

For hikers, hunters and camera buffs, a small, sturdy day pack is hard to beat. They are versatile, easy to carry, and serve double duty by carrying camera gear, extra clothes and a hearty lunch. Day packs weigh next to nothing, so you can stow as many components as you can comfortably tote. Look for strong construction, reinforced stitching at stress points, padded straps and brightly colored fabric. The color makes you just a little easier to find—and helps keep the kit from disappearing if you set it down and wander off to shoot a picture or explore a canyon.

Fanny packs or belt packs may be even better if you dislike having something over your shoulders or carrying weight up high. A good belt

pack will hold almost as much as a small day pack, with practically no restriction to your mobility. Watch for sturdy construction, a rather boxy design, a rugged, full-length zipper and a wide belt with a secure buckle.

When you are searching for just the right container for your survival gear, don't forget your pockets. They offer exceptional convenience and there is practically no chance you will ever lose *all you*r survival items. That can happen with single-container kits. Backpackers are especially prone to losing survival kits. Their packs are a virtual home away from home, but there is always a tendency to park the pack for "just a minute" to make a short side trip, check a spectacular view, or just to flex some weary muscles. All too often that's when problems occur. It is easy to get hurt or be unable to locate your pack and be left without supplies.

By scattering survival items throughout your clothing you can avoid the lost-kit syndrome. Remember, the best survival kit is not necessarily the one that is most complete—it is the one you have with you when you need it.

The one time I really needed a survival kit, I lost it in an aircraft accident. The extra items I had scattered throughout my pockets proved to be quite adequate. It may be wise to put some of your eggs in different baskets, especially if you fly or if you carry a backpack that is cumbersome enough to be set aside occasionally.

For aircraft survival kits it is best to split your equipment at least two ways. Put the bulky items in a kit, stowed in the baggage compartment or under a seat, but carry your critical *personal* survival items *on your person*. Often a forced landing ends up with a fire that prevents recovery of the survival kit. Then it's awfully nice to have the really important stuff fastened to you when you run from the wreckage.

Auto survival kits are the most versatile of all. Weight is usually no object, so anything that will hold the gear you need and not rattle around will fill the bill. Old suitcases, duffel bags, cardboard boxes or small packs work just fine. Even the best of car trunks often leak dust, so it is good to use a container that will protect your spare clothes and survival gear. In four-wheel-drive rigs the kit should be fastened to the floor or seats so it doesn't fly around and hurt someone. A sturdy plywood box bolted to the floor and secured with a padlock is hard to beat. You will need large, sturdy water containers in any vehicle.

Bicycles and motorcycles call for a "hybrid" approach. You can use saddlebags or other attached containers, but if your bike is a stripped down, lightweight model, it may be best to carry the essentials in a belt pack or day pack.

A good survival kit for horseback requires some thought. Saddle-bags are an obvious solution, but you may lose your horse in the same mishap that gets you into a survival situation. Saddlebags do you no good on a scared horse that you can't catch. I've used a small day pack and find it quite comfortable. Fanny packs work well too. They have to be worn a bit higher than usual, but they rest on the cantle of the saddle with no problem.

The toughest part is your water supply. Water is heavy and containers tend to bounce and chafe with the movement of the horse. However, it is risky to fasten your entire supply to the saddle. You may have to accept some discomfort and carry at least part of your water supply in your pack or in a canteen slung over your shoulder or on your belt.

Once you have settled on a container that can go along on every outing, there is a tendency to start stuffing it with goodies. There is also a danger of being swept up in a wave of survival gimmickry to the point that the proven lifesaving devices get left out in favor of flashy, well-advertised gadgets with limited usefulness. One way to avoid the problem is to use a shopping list approach to insure you cover all the essentials, then buy only what you have preselected.

By dividing your list into categories, you can further direct your thinking and buying to insure you do not ignore basics in favor of nice-to-have goodies. You will need body protection, shelter, fire-starters, signaling aids, some body maintenance items, and possibly something for your morale. Let us take them in that order and look at some compact, effective and (in most cases) cheap ways to cover these needs. Select items from each list that meet your needs and fit into your kit.

Survival Kit Item Checklist

Shelter Building Items (Chapter 3)

- ❑ Garbage or leaf bags (big, bright and heavy)
- ❑ Tube tent (folds to handkerchief size)
- ❑ Nylon cord
- ❑ Wire saw
- ❑ Sturdy knife

Fire Building Aids (Chapter 4)

- ❑ Firestarter
- ❑ Butane cigarette lighter and spare flints
- ❑ Waterproof case with matches
- ❑ Candles (thick, high melting point)
- ❑ Commercial gel or tablets

Signaling Aids (Chapter 5)

- ❑ Flares
- ❑ Signal mirror
- ❑ Police whistle
- ❑ Flashlight
- ❑ CB radio or cellular phone

Body Protection Items (Chapter 9)

- ☐ Sun hat
- ☐ Stocking cap
- ☐ Sunglasses
- ☐ Sunblocking lotion
- ☐ Jacket, wool shirt, sweater
- ☐ Wool socks
- ☐ Sturdy boots
- ☐ Plastic garbage bags (for use as a raincoat)
- ☐ Insulated underwear

Body Maintenance and Personal Items

- ☐ Aspirin or similar pain remedy
- ☐ Prescription medications
- ☐ Large clear plastic bags (for collecting water)
- ☐ Comb (helps in removing cholla cactus)
- ☐ Coins (for pay phones)
- ☐ Water purification tablets
- ☐ Small sharpening stone
- ☐ Antiseptic ointment
- ☐ First aid kit
- ☐ Needles and thread
- ☐ Pencil and paper
- ☐ Pocket knife
- ☐ Insect repellent
- ☐ Safety pins
- ☐ Tweezers
- ☐ Soap

☐ WATER!!! Carry all you can.

(You will need at least a gallon per person per day.)

Vehicle Support Items

Carrying the right things in your vehicle can prevent most survival situations. A vehicle support kit and cautious, thoughtful driving are your best insurance.

- ❏ Fuel (Do not carry cans of fuel inside the vehicle.)
- ❏ Oil (several quarts)
- ❏ Tire chains
- ❏ Tire pump
- ❏ Ax
- ❏ Shovel
- ❏ Extra fan belts
- ❏ Carpet scraps (for traction)
- ❏ Tool kit
- ❏ Spare hoses and clamps
- ❏ Stop-leak for radiator
- ❏ Tow strap or rope
- ❏ Gloves
- ❏ Electrical tape
- ❏ Wire
- ❏ Jack pad (plywood, one foot square for sandy areas)
- ❏ Vehicle repair manual
- ❏ Maps
- ❏ Global Positioning System (GPS)

Morale Items

- ❏ Sugar cubes
- ❏ Concentrated food bars
- ❏ Dried fruit
- ❏ Hard candy
- ❏ Bouillon (Coffee and tea are diuretics and tend to dehydrate you. **Do not** use unless water is plentiful.)
- ❏ Inspirational reading material and *THIS BOOK*!!!

Give some real thought to your survival kit. Then use it! Replenish it as necessary and make it *your* kit. The more personal it becomes, the better it will serve you. Finally, NEVER, NEVER go off without it.

But What About Food?

Food is critical to your survival—but not in the short term. In most emergency survival episodes, the food you eat before you go afield is more crucial than anything you might forage.

In a desert survival situation, food is one of your last worries. Yet more has been written over the years on foraging and snaring than on getting rescued.

Two factors tend to relegate survival food to the "nice to have" category. First, your body stores quite an impressive amount of food energy. People have lived in excess of a month without eating. Even under rigorous conditions, survival histories of two to three weeks without food are well-documented. Second, long-term survival episodes are becoming more rare each year. If you will just file a flight plan, there is little chance you will ever have to survive for more than a few days and you can do that on internally-stored food.

In the short term, however, food is important to your spirits. It can be a strong psychological factor and improve your efficiency and endurance. That means if you can eat, you will be able to do more to help yourself and "enjoy" your survival experience more. So, contrary to popular opinion, food is not vital to short term survival—but it is worthy of mention.

First, insure that you begin with a "full tank" of energy. That means eating a well-balanced diet day to day.

Second, carry some food with you. Modern technology has made that very convenient to do. A whole host of compact, nourishing food products have appeared on grocer's and camping outfitter's shelves in recent years. It is no longer necessary to carry a soggy, squashed sandwich to replenish your energy supply during a long day away from home. It's far easier now to slip a few granola bars, breakfast bars, some freeze-dried trail packets, or a sack of trail mix into your pockets, pack or vehicle. They'll provide a fairly well-balanced snack that tastes good and helps keep you at peak efficiency all day long—and beyond.

There is one caution to be observed whenever you eat away from your usual haunts. You have to have water to digest what you eat. If you eat when water is scarce, you will dehydrate yourself. Food can actually worsen your condition if you eat without drinking adequate water.

Plants

The easiest way to provide yourself something to eat is to forage for edible plant life. In most desert areas, you can find plants that contain some of the nutrients you need—but there is a problem.

A tremendous variety of plants, edible and inedible, can be found in desert areas. Unless you devote years to their study you are not going to become an expert on edible plants, except possibly in a small area or zone. Certainly, there are a few plants that are so delicious and nutritious and so widespread that they are worthy of memorizing. There are many others that are good for you, but it takes time and practice to identify them. Some have poisonous look-alikes. Others are safe when cooked but are poisonous raw. Still others have both edible and poisonous parts.

The point of all this is simple. Unless you are a plant specialist by trade or hobby, don't depend on being able to identify all of the edible or poisonous plants—even in your own local area.

Fortunately, that does not mean you will have to shy away from eating plants in a survival situation. If you learn and follow a few simple rules, you can have the advantages of eating things that grow from the ground without danger of poisoning yourself. You do not even have to recognize the plants by name or appearance.

No Mushrooms

Stay away from fungi as survival food. Many of them are downright delicious, but as a group they share two big drawbacks. They offer little food value, and there is no sure way to tell the good ones from those which are poisonous—except by visual identification. Learning to select the right ones—without fail—is a big challenge. Some toxic mushrooms are deadly, and no antidote will reverse or stop the damage they can do.

Mushrooms and related fungi are not survival fare!

No Beans or Peas

The legume family is not to be trusted. Many of them are poisonous, and even those we use regularly can become poisonous under certain conditions. When they grow in the same spot year after year (as they do in the wild), they pick up and concentrate minerals from the soil; and each generation becomes more toxic.

Look Out for Bulbs

Unless you can positively identify a bulb as edible, leave it alone. There are some which could really end your survival experience. There are two exceptions to the positive identification rule for bulbs. One is the edibility test which follows. The other involves similarities. Bulbs that look, smell and taste like onions or garlic are edible.

Avoid Weird-Looking Plants

Hairy leaves or stems, spines, thorns, or shiny leaves are all danger signs. Do not eat them. Some edible plants have these same characteristics, but by avoiding all of them, you help insure your safety. If a plant irritates your skin when you touch it, do not eat it. Skin irritation does not necessarily mean the plant is poisonous, but it may, so why take a chance?

Avoid Milky-Sapped Plants

Milky sap normally indicates a poisonous plant, and a survival situation is no time to look for exceptions to the rule.

No White, Yellow or Red Berries

Again, you will pass up some perfectly safe fruit by avoiding white and yellow berries but will avoid a much larger group of dangerous ones. If you eat an unidentified red berry, you are taking about a fifty-fifty chance that it is poisonous. With blue or black berries you are pretty safe. Only a few are toxic. If you do not recognize a dark-colored berry, but feel you need to eat it, use the test described below. One happy note on berries—all the aggregated ones are edible. So, if you find some that are made of individual juice cells, like the common raspberry, go ahead and eat.

Edibility Test

The rules are conservative and overly protective, but there are plenty of plants left to choose from. Some of them can cause you grief, even though they fit none of the categories listed above. You can separate these from the harmless ones by using a simple edibility test. It is time consuming but effective. Actually, even the time involved can be a plus factor in a survival situation. Boredom can be a bigger problem than lack of food.

First, select one plant that is plentiful and easy to recognize. There is no use testing something too rare to provide a useful quantity of nutrition, or one easily confused with something else. Also, the test must be run all the way through on a single plant before beginning a new one.

Second, select the part of the plant that appears most palatable to you. Remember, some excellent food plants have toxic parts. Crush some of it and check the juice or sap. If the sap is clear, touch a drop to your tongue, and be alert for danger signals such as a bitter taste, a numbing sensation on your tongue, lips or mouth, and nausea.

Assuming this initial contact is successful, you're ready to try step three. Put a teaspoon-sized chunk of the plant into your mouth and chew it without swallowing for five minutes. Be alert for the same danger signs as in step two. If there are still no ill effects, swallow the sample and wait eight hours.

If you still feel all right at the end of the wait, try a larger portion of the plant. About half a cup is fine. These quantities are not critical. Again, wait eight hours. If you don't get sick or suffer numbness, burning or itching, consider that part of the plant edible—but do not gorge yourself on it. Go easy.

You will have to repeat the test for each part of each plant you select as a potential survival food for each method of preparation. If you test the plant parts raw, eat them raw. If you boiled them first, eat them that way. Plant poisons react differently to various methods of cooking.

If at any point, your test shows the plant will cause you grief, you have three choices: give up and try another plant, switch to a different part of the plant, or try preparing it some other way.

Boiling is one effective way of eliminating undesirable effects of plant toxins. If your test netted you nothing more than a sore mouth or a bellyache, but you still feel the plants you tested are the best potential ones around, try to neutralize the poison.

Boiling will not neutralize all plant toxins—or there would be no need for the taste test. However, boiling is effective on about half of the common poisons found in plants.

Animals

All mammals are edible. Obviously, unless you are surviving with the aid of some very special equipment, you will find it more practical (and safer) to zero in on little critters.

The snare is the simplest way to catch small mammals. To make one, you need a length of brass or steel wire with a small "eye" twisted into one end. Strong cord will work, too. Push the free end through the eye to form a loop that is just large enough to admit the head of your quarry. Secure the end to a tree, log or rock and suspend the loop at the level your quarry carries its head.

It does little good to place snares at random. To be effective, they should be set in a heavy traffic area. For this reason they are most useful with "trail" animals, such as rabbits or squirrels. You can multiply your odds by funneling the animal toward the snare by making a twig or brush barrier across the trail, on either side of the snare.

You can get as fancy as you wish—there are books to explain exotic snares. However, there are just two vital rules in using snares: set them on trails or heavy traffic areas, and set lots of them! Do not rely on one or two snares.

Another very simple way to catch small animals and birds is the box trap. Generations of American kids have caught all sorts of critters in these—from the neighbor's cat to hapless sparrows. Under survival conditions you may have to make your own box. It is easy to do. Just tie sticks together, log cabin fashion and add a top of parallel sticks. String, thread from your clothes, strips of bark or grass will work for tying.

To set a box trap, place the box open side down and prop up one edge with a stick that is just long enough to admit your prey. Place some appropriate bait under the box and tie a string to the stick. Then step back out of sight with string in hand and wait—and wait. When your supper steps under the box to test the bait, yank the string, pulling out the prop and drop the box. You can also use a heavy flat rock or log in place of the box—then you have a manually triggered "deadfall."

Birds

Meat-eating birds can be caught with a fishhook embedded in a scrap of meat tied with several feet of string to an anchor point. Most other birds are quite easy to catch in a box trap.

Reptiles

Snakes, lizards, turtles and frogs are all edible, and most are quite tasty. You can catch most species by whacking them on the head with a stick. Since some snakes and a few lizards have poisonous bites, it is wise to take some precautions.

First, never hunt for snakes where the snake has the advantage. Do not climb over rocks or crevices or put your hands or feet down where you cannot clear the area first. You have to know that you can see the snake before it can strike you. Second, cut the head off any snake or lizard as soon as you are sure it is dead. Be careful, the fangs of a dead reptile are just as potent as those of a live one. One scratch can ruin your day.

Skin snakes, lizards and frog legs, then cook them any way that suits you. Turtles are easiest to cook by simply laying them on their backs in the coals. The shell becomes the pot.

If you haven't tried rattlesnake, you're missing a real delicacy. A friend of mine served one on a pilaf of rice at a formal buffet. It was the hit of the meal—even after the guests learned what they were eating.

Fish

If you are near water and your kit includes hooks and line, you can find bait and catch fish. You may have to spend a lot of time and experiment with many kinds of bait, but eventually you will entice something to bite. Remember, you are not trophy fishing. A four-inch bottom fish will taste just as good in a survival shelter as a fifteen-inch brook trout. Persistence pays. If one spot or one bait is unproductive, try another.

In small streams it is often possible to chase fish into shallow spots and catch them by hand or whack them with a tree branch.

Insects

That's right, bugs! Insects are probably your easiest source of survival nutrition if three conditions are met: 1) you have adequate drinking water, 2) the weather and your location make them available, and 3) you can quell any aversion you might feel toward eating them. You may have little control of the first two, but aversion can be conquered.

Insects are protein-rich and a popular food source in many parts of the world. Nearly all of them are "clean" and most are quite tasty. You will probably like them best roasted or fried, but if you aren't able to cook them, you can eat them raw. It pays to be cautious with raw ones, though.

Jim was attending a survival course when he noticed his instructor sitting cross-legged near a mound, eating something. "Mmm, termites. Here, have some, Jim," he offered. Jim was squeamish, but was not about to show it. He picked up a single termite and bravely popped it into his mouth—and promptly let out a yell. "The little devil bit me," he howled.

That ended Jim's aversion to insects. He sought revenge by first biting the head off every termite he could catch. If you must eat insects raw, Jim's method is a good one. "He who bites first…"

Ants, bees, grubs, grasshoppers, hairless caterpillars, and termites are all edible and highly nutritious. To roast, lay them near fire coals and cook until crispy. You can find them almost anywhere by turning over rocks, prying open rotting wood, opening anthills. Hunt insects early in the morning, while they are still cold and sluggish.

A few insects are somewhat poisonous; so if you venture beyond the common ones listed above, use the taste test described in the plant section of this chapter.

You can take advantage of natural food in the desert.

▲ Be observant.

▲ Consider anything that grows, walks, crawls, flies or swims as a potential food source.

▲ Be prepared to eat anything you find!

These basics about food will help you hold body and mind together while you attend to the business of getting rescued. If you are intrigued with living off the land by "root cooking and bug eating," there are many manuals and guides available. This book's primary emphasis is on getting you home.

Dealing with
Injuries and Illness

Several years ago a brake failure in an old jeep thrust me into a survival episode about seventeen miles from an Arizona public highway. A sturdy pine tree stopped the runaway jeep just before it would have plunged over a cliff into the Salt River Canyon, but the impact left me with blood spurting from my head. It was obvious I had severed an artery. Fortunately, my partner knew what to do.

He pressed hard against my temples with the heels of his hands. The spurts diminished to drips, and in about ten minutes the bleeding had virtually stopped. Then he walked out for help. His knowledge had turned a very serious survival situation into an educational adventure.

Probably nothing complicates a survival experience as much as an injury. Yet many people become survivors simply because they get hurt. Even a minor injury in the outdoors can turn a pleasant afternoon into a dire emergency.

You can minimize the limitations of most injuries and some illnesses by taking simple but appropriate action. It's not likely that you will be able to cure serious problems, but you can control the impact of common injuries on your survival. The actions you take in your own behalf or to help an injured partner in a survival situation are not really first aid. Courses in first aid and Emergency Medical Technician (EMT) classes deal with what to do until a doctor can take over. First aid is geared to relatively short-term treatment intended to stabilize an injury until professional help can be obtained. There are two differences between first aid and "survival medicine." First, under survival conditions you don't know how long it will be until you can get professional treatment. Second, you may have to use or even misuse the injured part for higher priority problems like shelter building or signaling. You cannot make treating your injury your sole function, but you must minimize its impact on your situation.

Let's look at some common survival injuries and see what you can do.

Pain

The pain associated with many injuries may be serious enough under survival conditions to warrant attention as a separate problem. Individual sensitivity and reaction to pain varies tremendously. Identical injuries in two people may produce nearly disabling agony in one while the other suffers only minor discomfort.

An Air Force survival manual states that you can tolerate any amount of pain if your goals are high enough. That may be overstating it a bit, but keeping busy and concentrating on the business of getting rescued can certainly reduce the impact of pain.

Your body announces damage or disease by flashing a pain warning. It reminds you to rest that part. Under normal conditions this is good; but when your life depends upon your ability to deal with survival problems, you may have to ignore the warning. Survival case histories are full of instances where people did just that.

First, understand that pain is a signal and not dangerous in itself. Second, concentrate on what needs to be done. Stay busy and keep your goal in mind. You want to get home! So work at that. Do not cater to your pain when your survival is at stake. Finally, try to look upon your pain as a temporary discomfort that can be tolerated. Naturally, you want to avoid aggravating the pain or the injury that is causing it, but remember to "keep first things first."

Shock

Shock may be the result of heavy bleeding, severe pain, burns, allergies, infection or psychological factors such as the sight of an injury to yourself or someone else. Any of these causes may be present in a survival episode. The result is the same regardless of the cause. Blood circulation to the brain is disrupted and rather predictable symptoms appear.

If you have ever experienced shock, it is unlikely you will forget the symptoms. The light-headed, weak, half sick, unreal feeling is indelible. If you have never felt shock or if you are watching for it in someone else, here are the signs you can expect to see:

1. The skin will feel cold and clammy.
2. Breathing rate will increase and may be quick and shallow or irregular and gasping.
3. Pulse will be weak and rapid.
4. Nausea or vomiting is likely.
5. There will be some mental confusion.

There are later, more severe symptoms—but you have to catch and treat shock *before* they occur.

Regardless of the cause, you can use one standard treatment:

1. Control bleeding (if there is any).
2. Drink plenty of fluids. (But do not try to give them to someone who is unconscious.)
3. Lie down, preferably with the head slightly lower than the feet, and rest until the symptoms pass. (For a head wound, you elevate the feet without lowering the head.)
4. Stay warm. Put on extra clothes and if a sleeping bag is available, get into it.

Bleeding

Blood loss from a wound can usually be controlled by direct pressure. Certainly, that is the first method you should try. Take a clean pad (sterile if you have it) and press it firmly against the wound. Hold it there until the bleeding is controlled. You may have to wrap the pad in place to hold the pressure.

If direct pressure doesn't work or you can't reach the wound, you can apply pressure between the wound and the heart. Major arteries run very close to the surface at several points on your body. These "pressure points" offer an opportunity to restrict the flow of blood from the heart to the wound. You can use your hand to press against these arteries or you can push the pressure point against some padded object. The illustration on the following page shows where these pressure points are located.

If the wound is on an arm or leg and neither pressure on the wound nor pressure on the artery supplying blood controls the bleeding, a tourniquet is a last resort—a desperation move. It can save your life, but it may cost you the limb if rescue is delayed very long. Tourniquets are so effective in controlling the flow of blood that they starve the limb of virtually all circulation. The bleeding will stop, but so will the flow of life-giving oxygen.

If you leave the tourniquet in place, you may lose the limb due to prolonged lack of oxygen. However, if you release it, the rush of blood into the limb can reduce your blood pressure enough to send you into deep shock—the kind you cannot take care of yourself.

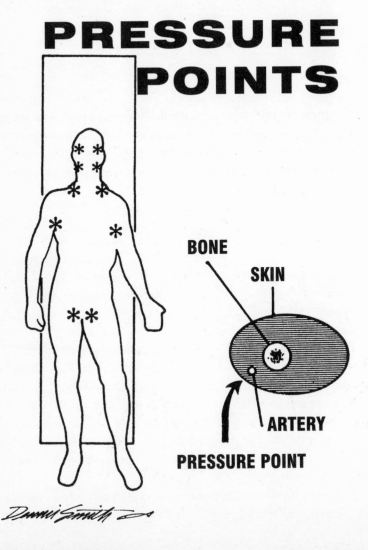

PRESSURE POINTS

BONE

SKIN

ARTERY

PRESSURE POINT

Fractures, Sprains, Strains and Dislocations

Although these injuries have little in common medically—other than involving the skeleton and its connective structures—they have similar effects on you as a survivor. All can cause severe pain, swelling, and lack of desire or ability to use the affected part. Regardless of the ultimate diagnosis, these injuries can deprive you of part of your survival equipment. Even a sprained finger can be quite a loss when you are trying to light a fire under life-and-death circumstances.

Fortunately, the survival treatment for all four structural injuries is the same; there is no need to attempt an exact diagnosis. Leave that to the doctor when you get home. Do not try to "set" a fracture or "reduce" a dislocation. That's a job for a professional. Just immobilize the injury, and you will reduce the pain and prevent aggravating the problem.

Hand, arm and shoulder injuries can often be immobilized sufficiently with a simple sling. You can make one from your belt, lengths of rope, a piece of clothing—anything that will form a loop around your neck to support the damaged arm. With a little patience you can make a sling with one hand. One survivor even improvised slings for two broken arms. He used his teeth to tie the knots.

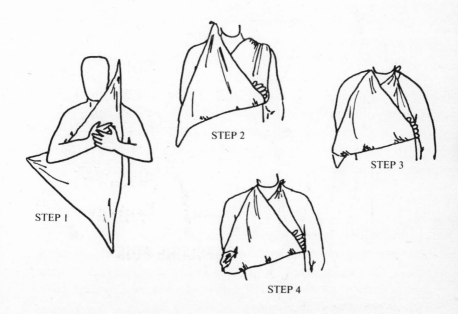

STEP 1

STEP 2

STEP 3

STEP 4

Splints are effective for protecting structural injuries. You can fashion splints from small poles, tree limbs, cardboard or any rigid or semi-rigid object you can find. An injured leg may be temporarily splinted against an uninjured leg. Always pad the splint to prevent painful pressure or abrasions. Use cloth strips or tape; *never* use cord or twine as it may constrict circulation. Tie the splint in place with plenty of snug knots. Treat any wound in the area prior to applying the splint.

The purpose of splinting is to immobilize the joints both above and below the injury. If that is not possible, try to prevent any movement in the injured area. If a foot or ankle is involved, keep your shoe or boot on.

When you have to get around with an injured leg or foot, a cane or crutch is a big help. A padded, forked pole will serve as an emergency crutch.

Blisters

Friction, thermal burns, sunburns or stinging plants can cause blisters. All are potential hazards for survivors. A blister is essentially a protective reaction over an injury. It should be left intact. Do not open or drain the fluid from blisters. Protect them with a clean dressing or padding.

Better yet—avoid blisters by protecting yourself from the things that cause them. Be extra careful and cautious in a survival situation. When you feel a sock or boot rubbing, stop and fix the problem or stay off your feet for a while. Keep your feet dry; if necessary, take time to dry and air them periodically. Avoid hand blisters while using your knife or building a shelter. If a spot gets tender and sore, either pad it, switch hands, use a different grip, or rest awhile. To prevent blisters caused by exposure to sun, plants or heat, you have to protect your skin from the causes.

Sun Blindness

Prolonged exposure to bright light can damage your eyes and cause needless pain and discomfort. When you feel yourself squinting excessively use sunglasses. If you don't have them, either get out of the glare or make a pair of goggles. A strip of heavy cloth, a piece of thin bark, or even a bit of aluminum foil will work. Just cut or tear a piece about an inch and a half wide by six inches long and cut narrow slits horizontally so they will be centered over each eye. Then tie the strip over your eyes, Lone Ranger style.

Sun blindness is sneaky. If you fail to protect yourself, you may still get through the day without apparent trouble—only to be struck by burning, watery eyes, poor vision and headache after sundown. When those symptoms appear, it's too late. You can then expect a day of discomfort or blindness. All you can do then is protect your eyes from further exposure to light by bandaging them or by staying in your shelter. The application of cold compresses will ease the pain.

Sun blindness will spoil the finest day in the outdoors. In a survival situation it is disabling. When you first notice excessive squinting, act!

Burns

Probably no survival injury is as serious or as difficult to deal with as a severe burn. With anything more than a simple first-degree burn (where the skin is only reddened), dehydration, and infection are likely to occur in that order. The shock is caused by pain and trauma to the circulatory system near the burn. Dehydration caused by loss of body fluids in the burned area will require a much higher than normal intake of water. The loss of skin and the favorable conditions for bacterial growth pose a threat of infection which cannot be controlled in a survival situation; however, infection will not likely be a factor for a day or so.

You are quite limited as to what can be done for a burn without sterile conditions and some medical gear. As a result, it makes little difference what the medical diagnosis of the severity of your burn might be. There is not much point in trying to determine whether you have a first, second or third degree burn—you will have to treat them all pretty much the same.

Your first move should be to cool the burned area. Do not waste time! Plunge the burned part into cold water or anything you have that will chill the injury without further damage (NO ICE). Cooling prevents harm from residual heat in the tissues. Unless you get the temperature back down to normal quickly, tissue damage may continue for several seconds after the heat source is removed.

Clean the burned area with soap and water, but be gentle. You do not want to compound the injury by disrupting damaged tissue. Do everything you can to keep the burned area clean and protected. Cover the burn with the most sterile dressing you can contrive. Boiled clothing or commercial dressings from a first aid kit are ideal.

Pain will be a problem you will have to deal with. If you're not allergic, aspirin may help the pain and will also help prevent swelling. Be alert for signs of shock. Even if no shock symptoms occur, avoid salt and start drinking more water than you think you could possibly need. Water will help fight shock and will also ward off the dehydration that normally follows a burn.

Diarrhea

Common diarrhea is quite prevalent under survival conditions. It may be caused by nervous tension, by eating unfamiliar foods, or by intestinal infection from contaminated water. In any case it is uncomfortable at best and debilitating when it is severe. It causes dehydration which can only be combated by drinking what may seem like an excess of fluids.

Most diarrhea is relatively easy to control—even without access to a pharmacy. Just eat fresh (but cool) natural charcoal from your campfire. The taste is not unpleasant since all the pitch and cellulose are burned away. A couple of tablespoons will help get you back in control.

Fever

Like pain, fever is a symptom of some other problem, but it can be a survival problem in itself. If you have aspirin, take it according to directions for some relief. Drink plenty of fluids. Fever can be a symptom of dehydration.

Snakebite

If you get bitten by a venomous snake and cannot get professional medical attention, your best bet is to make every attempt to remain calm, drink plenty of water and seek professional treatment as quickly as possible. Do not rush around—that will increase the circulation of venom in your bloodstream. Tourniquets and cut-and-suck kits are no longer recommended.

Other Bites and Stings

Lizards:
Only two venomous lizards are found in North American deserts, the Gila Monster and the Mexican Beaded Lizard. Both are relatively sluggish and non-aggressive. There is little chance of being bitten if you watch where you put your hands and feet. Treatment is the same as for snakebite. Don't panic and drink lots of fluids.

Scorpions and Spiders:
Avoid these critters by keeping your hands out of cracks, crevices, and the underside of rocks, boards, etc. All scorpions and spiders are poisonous to some degree, although human deaths are relatively uncommon. The bites of two spiders, the Black Widow and Brown Recluse, are dangerous to humans.

Stinging Insects:
In the United States, stinging insects like bees, wasps, velvet ants, hornets, and yellow jackets cause more deaths than snakes, usually to people who are allergic to them. If you are allergic to stings, your physician may recommend that you carry a bee sting kit. Follow the doctor's directions on its use. If you are not allergic to stinging insects, treat their stings by immediately scraping (not pulling) the stinger away if it has been left behind. If you try to pull it out you will squeeze the poison sac and increase the dose. Treat for pain with a cold pack if you can.

Many survival injuries and illnesses can be prevented by keeping yourself and your camp clean and neat. That sounds trite, but it is true. The chance of getting hurt is greatly lessened when you keep everything in its place and use all your survival tools properly. By merely washing yourself and your clothes frequently, even when that seems like a very low priority item, you can reduce the odds that you will aggravate your survival situation by getting sick.

If you get hurt or ill in spite of your best efforts, remember, *your ultimate goal is to get home.* That must govern all of your efforts and decisions. With that in mind, it is up to you. *You're the doctor.*

13

What If

There is one simple, effective way to sharpen your survival skills and increase your outdoor enjoyment. It's free, it's fun, and it doesn't cost you one minute of your recreation time. The technique is so effective that it has become a basis for major portions of the emergency training of military and airline flight crews. These professionals sharpen their thinking, procedures, problem solving, and motor skills in flight simulators. Instructors present emergencies and the crews solve them in real time. The whole program develops a "what if" thought process.

Flight instructors instill similar patterns in their students when they pull the throttle to idle unexpectedly and call "forced landing." The student pilot has to find a place to put the airplane down. About the third time that happens, you start thinking, "What if that louse pulls the power off now—where will I land this thing?" Strangely, this does not degrade your thinking about the minute-by-minute business of flying, but it does make you aware of potential landing spots along your routes of flight.

You can do the same thing to yourself. Practicing "what if" can improve your ability to deal with real emergencies. In addition, you can virtually eliminate the initial rush of panic that often accompanies unexpected trouble in unfamiliar surroundings.

Suppose you are driving your car through a rather isolated piece of desert and ask yourself, "What if the radiator hose breaks and I lose all the engine coolant?" or "What if I blow a tire and smack into that embankment, damaging the front suspension?" Several things may happen. You might answer yourself, "Ridiculous! Nothing is going to happen. I've driven for years without being stalled along the road." However, if you are persistent and play the "game," you will start noticing things you may have been ignoring. You may remember the

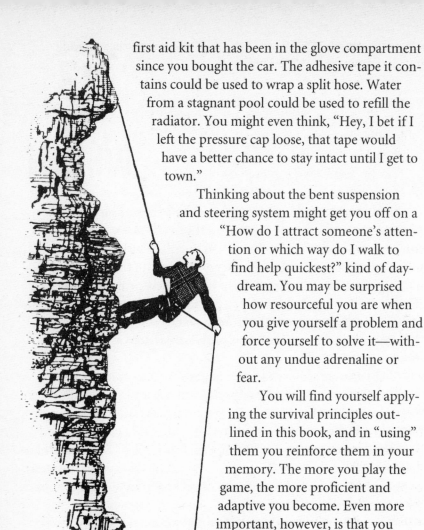

first aid kit that has been in the glove compartment since you bought the car. The adhesive tape it contains could be used to wrap a split hose. Water from a stagnant pool could be used to refill the radiator. You might even think, "Hey, I bet if I left the pressure cap loose, that tape would have a better chance to stay intact until I get to town."

Thinking about the bent suspension and steering system might get you off on a "How do I attract someone's attention or which way do I walk to find help quickest?" kind of daydream. You may be surprised how resourceful you are when you give yourself a problem and force yourself to solve it—without any undue adrenaline or fear.

You will find yourself applying the survival principles outlined in this book, and in "using" them you reinforce them in your memory. The more you play the game, the more proficient and adaptive you become. Even more important, however, is that you form a habit of acting rationally and constructively in an emergency. Nothing prevents panic like taking control of a situation. The more you practice taking charge of hypothetical (but realistic) emergen- cies the better you will perform in real cases.

Chuck, Marian and Susan buried their four-wheel-drive rig to the bumpers in a concealed, water-soaked clay vein at the bottom of a steep creek bed. They were about thirteen miles from a town and about half of that from a ranch. It was raining and cold wind whistled down the canyon. Chuck had "what ifed" a similar scenario while cruising down an interstate highway.

When prying with a long pole failed to budge the vehicle, and jerry-rigging the winch to pull the Toyota backwards broke the cable, he had already used two of the steps from his "what if" practice. Mending the cable with a knot almost worked, but the shear pin in the winch snapped. Frustration!

The three stranded explorers were still following steps from their mental practice. Marian suggested the CB radio. Chuck had dismissed that option earlier because of the deep canyon with signalblocking ridges on both sides. She tried anyway. After a few calls with no answer, a rancher with the appropriate call sign of "Clay Bank" crackled through the speaker. He said he knew the canyon, and within an hour the family was on their way, thanks to his big four-wheel-drive truck.

The point of all this is that each step followed smoothly and logically as the preceding step failed. They had all been rehearsed before, even though the situation was new to all three survivors. If Clay Bank had not shown up, the trek to the highway would still have been safe and easy, because it too was pre-imagined.

The situation was not too different from the stuck pickup in the desert discussed in Chapter 6. Chuck and his passengers might have worked feverishly trying to free their stuck four-wheeler and used all their reserve energy while they got soaked and chilled. The combination would have almost certainly resulted in hypothermia and a critical survival situation. However, their games of "what if" had programmed them to act slowly, rationally and with a plan. You could say they avoided *real* trouble by *pretending* they were in trouble before the fact.

Gail's experience was similar. She was an avid backpacker and got away whenever she could from her job as buyer for a big department store. Gail liked to go solo, but she recognized the extra danger. She used her commuting time to plan her trips and to "what if" them thoroughly. During breaks along the trail, she kept her mind active and off her work by asking herself how she'd handle various emergencies.

When Gail broke her ankle, she was disgusted with herself for being so clumsy. She was in pain, but she reacted as if she were using a script. She immobilized the ankle as best she could, crawled to a slightly overhanging rock face, built a fire and brewed some tea. Somehow the pain was not as bad while she was busy. By dark she had a shelter of sorts and enough wood to keep the fire going through the night—thanks to the crutch she fashioned from a forked tree limb. Except for the pain, she rather enjoyed doing something she had thought about for many months. There was no wasted motion—or emotion—no indecision and *no panic*. Having a plan of action prevented that.

Other hikers found Gail just before noon the next day. She rode off the hillside in a helicopter.

Playing "what if" tends to improve your confidence and to evolve a "will to survive" or "positive mental attitude." Volumes have been written on the importance of will and attitude, but the bottom line is this: you will think better and perform more confidently if you have prepared yourself physically, mentally and emotionally to deal with personal crises. You can do it by practicing when there is no emergency.

"What if" is a game where everyone wins!

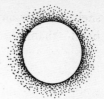

Index

Shivering 8-9, 49-50
Shock 74-75, 79-80
Shoes, see boots
Shortness of breath 7
Shorts 49, 51, 53
Signaling 23-28, 41, 52, 59
    CB radio 27, 35, 59, 85
    clothing 34, 52
    ELT 26-27
    fire 27
    flares 24, 59
    mirrors 25-27, 59
    radio 27, 85
    sound 26
    whistles 26, 59
Slings 77-78
Snakebites 69, 80
Snakes 69, 80
Snares 68
Socks 52, 60, 78
Solar stills 45
Sound, signaling 26
Spiders 81
Splints 78
Sprains 77-78
Stinging insects 81
Strains 77-78
Stress 39-40
Sun blindness 78-79
Sunburn 7, 51, 78
Sunglasses 53, 60, 78
Survival kits 55-61
Sweat, see perspiration

T

Tape 21
Temperature, body 3-5, 8-10, 80
Thirst 7
Tinder 18, 21
Tires 19, 24
Tourniquets 76, 80
Toxins 46, 68
Transpiration still 47
Turtles 69

U

Ultra-violet rays 51
Urination 7

V

Vaporizing fuel 17-18, 21
Vegetation still 46
Vehicle emergency items 52-53, 61
Vomiting 7, 75

W

Walking out 2, 11, 14, 30, 40
Water
    carrying 57-58, 60
    dehydration 5-8, 31, 39, 64, 79-80
    finding/making 43-47
Whistles 26, 59
Will to survive 10, 17, 86
Wind 12, 14, 51
Wool 50-51, 60
Wounds, head 73, 75

Other Books from American Traveler Press

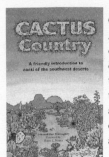

Cactus Country $7.95
A friendly introduction to cacti of the southwest deserts. Includes information and detailed drawings to help the reader locate and identify cacti. Humorous cartoons and recipes are also included.

Days of the West $12.95
An account of events that shaped the West during the 18th, 19th and 20th centuries. It answers the question, "What happened on January 1st?" Answers for the other 365 days of the year are also included.

Finding Gold in the Desert $4.95
The author shares techniques of finding placer gold and extracting gold from the deserts of the southwest through the process of drywashing. Includes plans for building a drywasher.

Grand Canyon Railroad $5.95
Fully illustrated guide to the railroad's history, ghost towns, explorations, volcanoes, wildlife, and railroad equipment. Filled with maps and illustrations, a must for railroad buffs.

Silly Saguaros $2.95
A lighthearted tribute to the giant saguaro and its many shapes and forms. This collection of 62 photographs offers fun and imaginative interpretations of what the saguaros might be saying or doing.

Easy Field Guide Series
$1.75 each
Desert

Arizona

California   New Mexico

Southwest

Ordering Information:

Shipping $2.50 on orders less than 4 pounds.
$5.00 for Priority Mail.
8.1% sales tax, but only on orders shipped within Arizona

If paying by check, send to:

American Traveler Press
5738 N. Central Avenue
Phoenix, AZ 85012
Call 1-800-521-9221 with Discover, MasterCard or Visa
Or visit AmericanTravelerPress.com and place order online